Praise

A Bigge

"Straddling the 'quiet depths of Zen' and the 'dynamism of corporate America,' suddenly thrown into the crucible of her husband's devastating accident and many months of constant caregiving, Pamela Weiss undergoes a mysterious transformation into wholeness. *A Bigger Sky* takes the reader on a profound, groundbreaking, and totally engaging journey of awakening and healing.

Bringing into vivid everyday life the model of the bodhisattva, she teaches us that nothing is outside of our spiritual practice and lays out the secret of how alchemy happens and true transformation takes root. She reveals a path of profound surrender, embodiment, and engagement with the world. In a time torn apart by patriarchal psychopathy, this book is a lion's roar to bring us back to our senses.

'Throw open the windows. Step into your life.'"

—KITTISARO & THANISSARA, coauthors of *Listening to the Heart: A Contemplative Journey to Engaged Buddhism*

"*A Bigger Sky* beautifully illuminates the power of the strong feminine and its essential role for us all in personal and planetary healing. In the process, Pamela Weiss shines an unflinching and much-needed light on the misogyny that has characterized the tradition's history and presents a contemporary way of integrating the masculine and feminine into a more complete spiritual path."

—FRANK OSTESESKI, author of *The Five Invitations*

"This is a wise, beautiful book. Pamela tells her story with complete transparency, describing the long journey she took to give herself the same compassion that she has gifted so many others. As I was reading, I felt myself soften to the original source so lucidly described in her writing. You will, too."

—ALLISON POST, coauthor of *The Gut Wellness Guide*

"A beautiful and courageous book for those new to the world of meditation and for those seeking a fuller expression of how the path can unfold. Genuine, heartfelt, and deeply inspiring."

—MATTY WEINGAST, author of *The First Free Women*

"In Pamela Weiss's beautifully written and heartfelt new book, she seamlessly weaves a variety of threads: her life story, a feminist take on Buddhist teachings, ancient myth, and hard-won wisdom from her spiritual path. Put together she creates a fascinating synthesis of pressing spiritual topics and personal discovery."

—DIANA WINSTON, author of *The Little Book of Being* and director of Mindfulness Education at UCLA's Mindful Awareness Research Center

"In *A Bigger Sky*, Buddhist teacher Pamela Weiss gives us an intimate account of her spiritual journey, honestly sharing both the rough waters and the wonderful, sustaining parts of the path. The profound wisdom gained is woven through her account, giving readers the benefit of her rigorous dedication. I highly recommend this engrossing account for anyone on a spiritual path."

—LAMA PALDEN DROLMA, author of *Love on Every Breath: The Power of Tonglen Meditation in Daily Life* and founder of Sukhasiddhi Foundation

"Pamela Weiss beautifully articulates the archetype of the human journey. But more than that, she expresses her own lived experience through journeys into Buddhist teachings, career, relationship, and identity, as well as the joys and sorrows of the only life we have to live."

—LARRY YANG, author of *Awakening Together: The Spiritual Practice of Inclusivity and Community*

"*A Bigger Sky* offers a vision of an American Buddhism that has worked through its psychological and sociocultural bypasses. First, it articulates an embodied feminine approach to awakening as a corrective to hyper-masculine transcendent narratives. Second, in confronting the structural affliction of racism, it signals a shift from individual to collective liberation. Practitioners who are birthing more inclusive and integrated forms of American Buddhism will find much inspiration here."

—ANN GLEIG, author of *American Dharma: Buddhism Beyond Modernity*

"Brilliantly and engagingly written, Pamela Weiss's personal journey through decades of Buddhist practice is a must-read for anyone interested in a contemporary spirituality as it unfolds—in the workplace, in the face of debilitating illness, in the midst of race and gender issues, and in the ongoing dynamic between personal love and spiritual vocation. *A Bigger Sky* is nothing short of an inspiration, especially for women seeking to challenge the status quo of religious orthodoxy."

—ROGER HOUSDEN, author of the bestselling *Ten Poems to Change Your Life* series and *Dropping the Struggle: Seven Ways to Love the Life You Have*

"With ruthless honesty, Pamela Weiss leads us through her life's journey—as a child with chronic illness, a devoted young Zen monk, a loving wife, a successful business woman, and always a deeply human being. Her yearning to awaken never leaves her, and with fierce persistence and love she transforms the obstacles on her path into the path itself. There are deep teachings in here—dive in!"

—BHIKKHUNI ANANDABODHI, cofounder of Aloka Vihara Forest Monastery and coauthor of *Leaving it all Behind*

"Pamela's lovely memoir is as full of wisdom as it is well written. Her spiritual journey takes us into uncharted territory, offering the intimations of a feminine approach to Buddhism. In its outlines, we begin to feel a sorely needed balance being restored."

—SANDRA MAITRI, author of *The Spiritual Dimension of the Enneagram* and *The Enneagram of Passions and Virtues*

"With engaging, intimate prose, Pamela Weiss illuminates how we can move through a world of increasing complexity while maintaining our values and aspirations. With deftness and insight, she challenges the relevance of androcentrism in Buddhism and gives voice to key female Buddhist figures. *A Bigger Sky* will benefit those who want to learn more about Buddhism as well as those struggling with its patriarchal origins."

—SEBENE SELASSIE, teacher and writer

"Pioneers are those who venture into unknown territory and settle. In *A Bigger Sky*, Pamela Weiss marries the 'settling' teachings of Buddhism with the unsettling truth of systemic inequality. Weaving stories of wise women— such as the Buddha's wife and Inanna of the ancient Sumerian myth—Weiss invites us to reflect on the universal process of descent, recovery, and restoration needed on the path of awakening, and inspires us to transcend the narrow definitions that have silenced women since antiquity. This book is heart medicine for our times!"

—SARAH POWERS, author of *Insight Yoga*

"Brave and inspiring. I am grateful to Pamela Weiss for taking me along as she shows how her suffering enabled her to fully engage with Buddhist practice, and how her Buddhist practice enables her to fully meet her suffering. I cheer her on as she finds her voice and her strength, and when I look up from these pages, I realize that she is the one who has cheered me on and given me courage."

—SUSAN MOON, author of *This is Getting Old* and coauthor of *What is Zen?*

"Pamela's writing is rich with wisdom, clarity, and heart. Her insights about her unique journey as a female practitioner in Buddhism and how she learns to integrate the jewels of Buddhist teachings in contemporary culture are illuminating. I highly recommend this new and insightful work that brings a fresh feminine perspective to ancient wisdom teachings."

—MARK COLEMAN, author of *From Suffering to Peace*

"*A Bigger Sky* is a wise, moving, exquisitely crafted book. It describes a path of intimacy that winds its way along the mountain roads of Zen practice, through lifelong illness, social histories, and awakenings to justice. Pamela Weiss shares stories of ancestral and contemporary women whose wisdom is pivotal to the relevance of the Buddhist tradition and the way to freedom for all beings. This is essential reading for Buddhists everywhere."

—KOSEN GREGORY SNYDER, senior priest at Brooklyn Zen Center and assistant professor at Union Theological Seminary

"What an extraordinary contribution to the groundswell of women's voices in Buddhism, past and present. Let's finally listen to these voices and let them lead us through delusion into the 'bigger sky' Weiss paints for us and that the world so desperately needs."

—MICHELLE LATVALA, Executive Director of Spirit Rock Meditation Center

A Bigger Sky

A Bigger Sky

Awakening a Fierce Feminine Buddhism

PAMELA WEISS

North Atlantic Books
Berkeley, California

Published by   Cover photo © gettyimages.com/4X-image
North Atlantic Books   Cover design by Nicole Hayward
Berkeley, California   Book design by Happenstance Type-O-Rama

Printed in the United States of America

A Bigger Sky: Awakening a Fierce Feminine Buddhism is sponsored and published by the Society for the Study of Native Arts and Sciences (dba North Atlantic Books), an educational nonprofit based in Berkeley, California, that collaborates with partners to develop cross-cultural perspectives, nurture holistic views of art, science, the humanities, and healing, and seed personal and global transformation by publishing work on the relationship of body, spirit, and nature.

North Atlantic Books' publications are available through most bookstores. For further information, visit our website at www.northatlanticbooks.com or call 800-733-3000.

Library of Congress Cataloging-in-Publication Data
Names: Weiss, Pamela, 1962– author.
Title: A Bigger Sky: Awakening a Fierce Feminine Buddhism / Pamela Weiss.
Description: Berkeley, California: North Atlantic Books, [2020] | Includes
    bibliographical references and index.
Identifiers: LCCN 2019052783 (print) | LCCN 2019052784 (ebook) | ISBN
    9781623174750 (trade paperback) | ISBN 9781623174767 (ebook)
Subjects: LCSH: Weiss, Pamela, 1962– | Buddhist women—United
    States—Biography. | Zen Buddhists—United States—Biography. | Women in
    Buddhism.
Classification: LCC BQ996.E57 W45 2020 (print) | LCC BQ996.E57 (ebook) |
    DDC 294.3082—dc23
LC record available at https://lccn.loc.gov/2019052783
LC ebook record available at https://lccn.loc.gov/2019052784

2 3 4 5 6 7 8 9 KPC 24 23 22 21

This book includes recycled material and material from well-managed forests. North Atlantic Books is committed to the protection of our environment. We print on recycled paper whenever possible and partner with printers who strive to use environmentally responsible practices.

For Teah

CONTENTS

PROLOGUE

I sat with my friend Teah and the abbot at a table in the abbot's living room. Sunlight streamed through the tall windows, branches tapped against the glass, bursts of ocean air rustled the grasses outside. Inside, a kettle whistled and the refrigerator hummed.

The abbot, my longtime teacher, placed three fist-sized teacups on a tray in the center of the table and gestured to us to take them. I turned the warmth of the cup in my hands. The sharp, grassy scent of sencha tea permeated the space.

As I gazed down into my teacup, Teah said, "I am going to do dharma transmission with Pam." She paused, and I imagined a slender smile flickering across the abbot's face. "But I do not want to ordain her," Teah continued. "Pam is not a priest. And I feel strongly that there needs to be a complete path of practice for laypeople living in the world."

Even as I kept my gaze averted, I felt the slip of the abbot's smile melt away. I listened to the grit in their voices as the conversation unfolded. Their words were polite, but the tone was heated, full of fire. I was silent, taking in the intensity of the moment.

I was the subject of their tense conversation, but the drama preceded me; it went back and back and back. Dharma transmission is the ceremony that confirms full authorization in Zen Buddhism. It would affirm my understanding and give me permission to pass on the lineage to others. Traditional Buddhist practice distinguishes between lay practitioners and monks or nuns. In Japan, the distinction is between priests and laypeople.

Until now, dharma transmission and the authority to pass on the lineage had been reserved for ordained priests. Which I was not.

When I fell into Zen practice at the age of twenty-five, it was very much like falling in love. After tiptoeing around the edges, I opened and gave myself completely, entering a monastery and devoting myself to a path that transformed my sadness and confusion and pain into something tender and useful.

For a while, I wanted to stay inside the walls of the monastery forever. But there was no path that would have allowed me to integrate my love of spiritual practice with my love of a real, flesh-and-blood human. So I was never ordained as a priest. Instead, I met my husband, left the monastery, and got married.

The experience of reentering the world was full of sharp edges. For years I felt cast out, heartbroken. I pressed my face against the windows of the temple and pounded on the doors, trying to find a way back in. Peering in from the outside, I was a jilted lover, filled with longing and regret.

I questioned my capacity to chart a path through the tangle of everyday life. Was it possible to engage in the world with open hands and an open heart without being consumed? I wasn't sure, but I knew I needed to find out.

In the decades after I left the monastery, my life straddled two worlds: the profound quiet and depth of Zen and the dynamism of corporate America. I understood that I would be breaking with tradition by completing dharma transmission as a layperson, but I wanted to lay the foundation for something new—to become a bridge for others to cross over.

I placed my teacup on the table, and the sound of clay striking wood made a sharp crack. Teah and the abbot both looked up. The volley of their conversation came to an abrupt stop.

"Um, can I say something?" I asked.

Before I had a chance to speak, the abbot leaned forward and cleared his throat. "If you do this," he said, looking directly at me, "the distinction between ordained priests and laity will blur and become confused." He reached his hands across the space between us and then slid them together, one on top of the other, to demonstrate his point.

A long, awkward silence ensued. Teah took a sip from her cup. The abbot folded his hands and placed them on the table in front of him, staring down.

"Actually, none of us knows what will happen," I blurted into the space. "I certainly don't."

I paused and looked the abbot in the eye. "I just want you to know that I am not doing this to be brash or disrespectful. I am deeply grateful for everything you have given me." I was surprised to hear the catch in my voice.

"This practice literally saved my life," I said in a near whisper.

For a long time, no one spoke.

When I looked up again, there were four wet, shining, blue eyes looking back at me.

PART I

Love Yourself Completely

1

SUFFERING AND
THE END OF SUFFERING

For some people, spiritual practice begins with dreams of serenity and bliss. For me, it started with a nightmare.

A rat scurries across my face, scratching my skin with twitchy, clawed feet. I reach up, grab the rat with my hand, and tighten my fingers around its squishy girth. The tiny animal kicks and squeals. I take an insulin syringe and begin stabbing the rat. I jab at its belly, again and again, until the squeaking and squirming stop and the dead rat droops heavy across my hand.

Jolted out of sleep, I looked down at my palms, expecting to find blood. I wiped my hands across the covers until my skin was pink and raw and then checked the bedsheets to see if they were smeared with streaks of red.

The violence of the dream echoed the battle raging inside me, a jagged line drawn between my mind and my body—between the veneer of the polished young woman I wanted others to see and the beasts clawing just beneath the surface. I had been living with type 1 diabetes for more than a decade, and I desperately wanted to be rid of it, to vanquish the disease and disorder that lurked inside me.

In the summer of 1973 I was sitting on the salmon-colored Formica counter of our kitchen in Berkeley when the doctor called. My mother lifted the phone handset from the wall and squeezed the slim beige unit between her curved neck and lifted shoulder.

"Hello," she said, and began to pace. The long, curled cord twisted as she circled the small space, wiping countertops with a towel as she listened. Lines of tension creased her face. She removed her glasses and wiped the back of her hand across her eyes. I slid off the counter and waited, hunched in the doorway, as she clicked the handset back onto the cradle.

"Mom," I said, leaning forward, "what's wrong?"

"You are diabetic," she announced. "The doctor wants you to check in to the hospital tomorrow. You need to go pack a suitcase. *Now.*"

I dragged my suitcase out of the closet and stared at the line of clothes swaying on their hangers. What does an eleven-year-old pack for the hospital? I grabbed blue jeans and pale purple sweatpants, my favorite fuzzy pink sweater and red-and-white striped shirt, a stack of clean cotton underwear, and three pairs of tube socks. I added spiral-ringed notebooks for each of my classes—English, math, biology, and Latin—my favorite green pen, and my toothbrush, toothpaste, and hairbrush. Before closing and zipping the bag, I grabbed my golden potbellied Pooh bear and tucked him inside.

My room at the hospital was dim and quiet, filled with flickering shadows. My roommate, Salma, lay in the bed next to mine. Her wide forehead and black hair were wrapped in white gauze. Her worried family crowded around her, whispering and twisting their hands.

I remember the clang of the trays on the meal carts and the sound of metal rings scraping on the circular bar above each bed when the nurse pulled the curtain shut between us. I heard, but could not see. Anxious voices rose and fell. In my imaginary story, I offer Salma a cough drop or extend a hand toward her across the cool linoleum floor. Our eyes meet; we smile. In the true story, I kept my gaze buried in schoolbooks, looking up only when someone in a white coat appeared.

There was a bone-thin boy who haunted the halls, dragging his IV pole behind him. I remember his pale face, sunken cheeks, and enormous eyes, how he dragged himself from room to room, peering in each doorway in silence. I pretended not to see him, looking away, but I felt his eyes on me. He wanted something I refused to give.

At night I could hear him howl, followed by a rush of footsteps and the muted murmur of words. How I wanted him to be quiet.

Each day a parade of people in white coats passed through my room to teach me new things I didn't want to know. "Insulin is the key that unlocks the door to let nourishment in," the nutritionist explained. "Without insulin, you will starve to death."

I practiced drawing liquid from a vial into a syringe. I pressed the plunger and injected the magic serum, first into the flesh of an orange, and later under my skin. I swiped my thigh with an alcohol swab, pinched the flesh, and pressed the plunger. It burned. I pretended it was happening to somebody else, to a sick girl in a hospital in Alaska or Brazil. I withdrew the needle and pressed down on the stinging spot. *Poor girl,* I whispered to myself. *She is very brave.*

"That wasn't so bad, was it?" the nurse asked.

"No," I lied.

I was not brave. I was scared. I wanted to go home. I wanted to go outside and play. I wanted to lie in the hallway of my house with my small body curled across the ribcage of my golden retriever, Rags, sifting through his silky hair, listening to him breathe.

My doctor's name was Ida Braun. She was a thin woman with wide knuckles and chapped lips. My mother told me, in a just-between-us whisper, "Her husband plays first violin in the San Francisco Symphony." I didn't know why that mattered, but I understood that Dr. Braun was an important person and very smart.

At our appointments, Dr. Braun took notes. A thin silver watch slid along her narrow wrist as she wrote. She spoke to me exactingly. "Record the results of your glucose tests in this logbook," she said. "Blue is low; bright orange is high." I understood: blue is good, orange is bad.

I wanted to be good.

Dr. Braun asked my mom, "Would you like Pam to meet with our social worker, Annie?"

I remembered passing Annie in the hallway. She was a soft, blonde woman with bouncy arms and round hips. She wore flowing pants, sturdy shoes, and colorful jewelry, and she always looked at me with a big smile.

"No, we don't need to see her," my mother replied.

On our way out, Dr. Braun squeezed my arm. "You are doing great," she said.

As my mother and I wound our way through the hospital hallways, I saw Annie's nameplate on her closed door: Annie Reynolds, LCSW.

"Mom, what's a social worker?" I asked.

"Social workers are for people with problems," she explained, "not for you."

I understood: I didn't have any problems. I was doing great.

At home, in the bathroom, a miniature chemistry set for tracking sugar in my urine rested on the shelf above the toilet: test tubes, an eyedropper, and mysterious tablets, thick and round, that made the liquid in the test tubes bubble and boil. For a stretch of days after each appointment with Dr. Braun, I diligently marked my results into the logbook.

But, discouraged by the barrage of bright orange results, I'd stop after a week, letting the test tubes and tablets gather dust. A day or two before the next appointment, I would fill in the logbook with a fictitious string of blues and greens, adding an occasional spike of orange—just enough bad to make it ring true.

At each appointment, I presented the logbook to Dr. Braun.

"This is excellent," she would say, creasing the page of the logbook with an unpolished nail. I watched the corners of her mouth tick up slightly. She looked contented, almost smug.

I smiled at her from my brown plastic chair, pleased she couldn't tell it was a lie.

"It's difficult when Pam has low blood sugar," my mother told her, belying my flaw-free version of the story. "She gets irritable and confused."

"Well, perhaps you could pack a box of raisins in her bag for school," Dr. Braun suggested. Then she looked at me with a satisfied expression and explained, "If you feel hypoglycemia coming on, just have a handful of raisins. That should do the trick."

Dr. Braun clearly knew nothing about the turmoil that descended on me when my blood sugar dropped—the sweaty palms and trembling knees. She didn't know about the frenzied animals let loose inside, how they scratched and pawed at my belly. *Feed me!* they'd snarl. How I'd grab at anything within reach: bags of peanut butter cookies, orange juice drunk straight from the bottle, jars of strawberry jam. How I'd swallow giant mouthfuls of unchewed food, lick my sticky fingers, and fall into a syrupy stupor with crumbs on my face.

"Okay," I said, nodding. A box of raisins. That should take care of everything.

Over the next ten years I went to visit endocrine experts, massage therapists, nutritionists, acupuncturists, personal trainers, and the occasional energy healer. But every time my blood sugar dropped, those inner animals began twitching and growling, and I didn't know how to appease them.

During that period, there were times when I ate only protein and leafy greens, or when I fasted and cleansed. There were other times when I secretly consumed pizza and beer and pints of ice cream with my friends, and then I crept into the bathroom, locked the door behind me, and threw all of it up into the porcelain bowl. I wept, raged at God, asked for forgiveness, felt sorry for myself.

Nothing worked.

After graduating from college I spent the summer studying Mandarin. I was set to travel to Wuhan University as the first-ever student representative in a new exchange program set up by my Chinese history professor, Vera Schwarcz. I loved studying Chinese history, and I was fascinated by Chinese medical concepts of illness and health, which offered a stark contrast to the Western medical model. Traditional Chinese medicine described diabetes as a "wasting and thirsting" disease caused by imbalanced energies in the body. To me, this felt truer and more hopeful than the Western medicine description and prognosis I had been given: your pancreas is broken, and it can't be fixed.

On a bright San Francisco morning I stood in line at the Chinese embassy with my visa application and passport in hand. I also carried a letter of explanation, translated into neat Chinese characters, from Peggy Huang, founder of the Diabetes Teaching Center at the Univesity of California, San Francisco. "Pam is diabetic and needs to carry insulin syringes," she wrote, hoping to help me avoid any mishaps with customs officials at the border.

The man behind the counter was framed in glass. He had thick, black-rimmed glasses, greasy hair, and a puffy face. I pushed my documents through the slot and watched as he scanned my passport and application. Then he pulled the letter from the envelope and read it through. When he came to the end, he made a short grunt and turned to walk away. A few minutes later he returned with a second man and handed him the letter. This man was thin, with pale lips and long arms. His eyes were impassive as he gazed at me and then began reading. I shifted my weight from side to side, hands in my pockets, waiting.

"Come back tomorrow," he said abruptly, pulling a dark gray shade down over the window to end the conversation.

I was rattled. My passport, application, and letter were now locked in the bowels of the consulate. When I returned the next morning, I waited in line again, taking in the sounds of a language I could not comprehend. The little Chinese I had learned during summer school was no match for the mysterious syllables that passed between the others also waiting in line.

As I approached the window, I made eye contact with the puffy-faced man from the day before. He registered my presence, barked "Closed for lunch!" and snapped the shade shut again.

I tapped on the window but got no response. With my stomach in knots, I turned and left, again without my passport or paperwork.

The third day I returned with a friend in tow. Together we waited, trading whispered lines of English above the background hum of Mandarin and Cantonese. As we approached the window, the clerk again slammed the shade shut. I tapped on the window: "You have my passport," I shouted through the glass. No response.

I widened my stance and planted myself, determined not to move. The line of people behind me began whispering. I looked from face to face for a sign of support, but no one met my gaze. Then a door I hadn't noticed before opened on the wall to my left. A man appeared, wearing a dark Western suit, shiny black loafers, and a red tie. "Follow me," he commanded, signaling my friend to take a seat.

I followed, listening to the sharp clicks of his shoes as we made our way down an ill-lit hallway. He ushered me into a large, dim room with walnut paneling and high, arching windows draped in long, red velvet curtains. A life-size portrait of Chairman Mao looked down on us from the far wall above the fireplace. The man motioned me to be seated on an old leather couch and then stood off to the side. A second man was seated in a chair directly in front of me. He had a dimpled chin and smelled of cigarettes. I thought I should probably be scared, or at least worried, but I wasn't.

"So you want to go to Wuhan?" said the man with the dimpled chin.

"Yes, I do," I replied with gusto.

"How long do you plan to stay?'

"One year," I told him, smiling. I felt as if I were reciting lines from a B movie, complete with a melodramatic soundtrack that only I could hear.

After peppering me with questions about the particulars of my stay, the man in the chair lifted himself to his feet and placed his manicured hands across his full belly. He looked at me directly for the first time.

"You are diabetic?" he demanded.

His question registered as an accusation or curse. The music stopped. My sense of humor seeped away. Suddenly I understood.

"But," I stammered, "I'm perfectly healthy. I can take care of myself. I won't get sick."

I knew it was no use. The conversation was over. I paused and fell into a teary silence.

"Here are your documents," he said, handing me a folder and escorting me outside.

Later I called Vera to let her know what had happened. Her voice sank as she said, "Chinese culture carries a very different sense of responsibility than we have in the West. If you go to China and get sick, it becomes a source of irreversible shame and dishonor to your hosts. I'll see what I can do, but I don't think it will be much."

The next day she relayed a message from the university in Wuhan: "We are very sorry to hear of Miss Weiss' illness. Please send another student."

Soon afterward I moved into an old Victorian walk-up with a room-mate named Sophie, who was a first-year law student. I took a nine-to-five job as a research assistant at a health care consulting firm. Every day I flashed my MUNI card, boarded the train, and traveled across the city, where I sat in a gray cubicle wearing pleated trousers, silk shirts, heeled shoes, and a string of fake pearls—my new professional wardrobe. All day I conducted interviews, crunched numbers, and wrote reports that I delivered to my boss, who then tossed them back onto my desk, covered in red ink.

"Run the numbers again," she would say. "We need the data to prove that our client can generate sufficient income to justify building a new facility."

Our clients were hospitals and physician groups vying for funds. My job was to prove they should receive money to launch an outpatient chemotherapy unit or cardiac catheterization lab.

I boosted the numbers by expanding the geographical reach to include the elderly and infants, until the data appeared to support the numbers the client needed. But the premise was absurd: how many infants or frail elderly would be clamoring for cardiac catheterization procedures? Almost none.

One dreary afternoon, my boss came to my office to get the latest report. When I handed it to her, she squinted at it and scrunched her face with disapproval.

"Run them one more time," she told me, poking at the page with a red pen. "We need to show an increase in net income over the next five years."

I took the red-lined pages in my hand, hung my head, and stared at the beige carpet. Then, no longer able to contain my exasperation, I looked up at her and asked, "Don't you think it would be better if we just told them the truth?"

"That's not what they're paying us for," she snapped, turning on her heel and marching back to her office.

As I watched her walk away, I was overcome with sadness as the realization hit me: *I can't do this anymore.*

I sat at my desk and dropped my head into my hands. When I looked up again and saw the report sitting on the desk, a wave of fury washed through me. I pictured myself sweeping everything off the desk onto the floor with a single angry brush of my arm, then emptying the drawers into a pile, unplugging the computer, and walking away. It felt like every cell in my body was screaming: *Leave now! Go! Get out!*

But I didn't know where to go or what else to do. So I booted up the computer and began revising the report.

That was the night I did battle with the rat in my dream—the night I woke, queasy and horrified, looking for blood on my hands.

When I pulled myself out of bed the next morning, I padded into the kitchen, weary and forlorn, sat down at the kitchen table across from Sophie, and told her everything: the rat, symbol of disease; the violence of my feelings; my fear and despair. As I spoke, I watched her eyes well up.

"Why don't you go see this guy?" she said, scribbling a phone number on a piece of paper. "He's a healer, visiting from Tibet. A monk. Maybe he can help you."

She slid the note across the table. I tucked it into the pocket of my pajamas without looking at it. That night, as I was getting ready for bed, I found the crumpled paper and set it on my nightstand. When I hit the snooze button on my alarm the next morning, I picked up the note, smoothed it out, and read it for the first time: Something-something Rinpoche, it said.

Before I was awake enough for doubt to kick in, I picked up the phone and dialed. The cheerful woman who answered offered me an appointment to see the visiting holy man the following week at the home of a Western Buddhist teacher in Marin County.

Rinpoche was a slight man with quiet, dark eyes. Draped in maroon and gold robes, he took my hands and fingers, and he pressed the veins of my wrist, using his fingertips to listen to the hum of my pulses. I sat still, scanning his face for answers: What did he feel? What did he hear? Could he fix me?

He looked up, drinking in the expectation in my eyes, and turned toward his translator. He spoke in soft, guttural bursts of sound. I leaned in, listening.

The translator began, "Rinpoche says, the most important thing for you . . ."

Yes?

"The main thing you need to do . . ."

I was perched at the edge of my seat.

"The most important thing you need to do," he told me, "is to love yourself completely."

I sat back, startled and annoyed. I wanted to shout, *But I am sick! I need help!* I wanted a remedy. I wanted words I could twist into a strategy or plan: *eat more broccoli, drink special tea, take a pill.*

Instead, his words cast a light on the self-loathing inside me.

I looked over at Rinpoche and watched him watching me. His gaze was filled with curiosity and kindness. His soft hands were folded in his lap, one placed gently on top of the other, as if he were cradling something tender and precious.

I didn't know how to do what he was asking. But whatever he was holding, I knew I wanted more of that.

After my meeting with Rinpoche, I looked up "Meditation" in the Yellow Pages and found my way to a local futon shop. I bought a firm, round cushion and placed it on the floor in my room. An eclectic stack of books piled up on the nightstand next to my bed: Stephen Levine, Ram Dass, Shirley MacLaine. I read about the benefits of meditation: "Thoughts don't disappear, but they float by like clouds in a broad sky." I liked the ideas, but I continued to tiptoe past my meditation cushion, seated in the corner. I glanced at it each morning and evening as I dressed and undressed. It stared back. I looked away.

This went on for several weeks, until I persuaded Sophie to accompany me to the morning meditation program at the local Zen center. The next

Saturday morning, we rang the bell and peered through the window, watching as a bald man in long black robes swept down the hall to let us in.

I remember the sounds: the *toc-toc* of the grandfather clock in the entryway, the deep reverberation of the bell, the monotone chanting. I remember the wafting scent of incense, the cool squish of tatami mats under my sockless toes, the beams of sunlight streaming through the long, arched windows.

The Zen center was compelling and odd—bald women and men wearing long, black gowns. My mind spun with apprehension and judgment. But I also felt a deep resonance. Something I didn't understand touched and thawed me. The people there carried a quality of stillness that easily erupted into smiles and laughter. I was struck by their presence, simple kindness, and candor.

I remember thinking, *Whatever it is they've got, that's what I want.*

Zen practice is formal. Movements and gestures are carefully choreographed: step over the threshold with the foot adjacent to the door hinges as you enter the meditation hall; hold your hands across your solar plexus, folding one into the other as you walk; press your palms together in prayer position as you bow to your cushion or chair, tilting gently at the waist.

For some people, the formality of Zen feels rigid. But for me, the precision of the external forms offered a safe container, lending a steadiness that allowed the chaos inside me to ease and unwind.

As weeks and months passed, I settled into a new rhythm—waking each morning at five a.m., slipping through the empty streets of the city with the early-morning traffic lights flashing and the windows of the apartment buildings still dark—to sit, chant, and bow. I signed up for one class and then another. I volunteered to help out in the kitchen. My physical shape began to transform—from concave, dense, and rubbery, to more poised and less defended. I began sweeping the floor of our apartment kitchen, scrubbing the toilets, and washing dishes piled in the sink.

"I like this new version of you," Sophie teased. I did too.

I was delighted to take up a new vocabulary, sprinkling my sentences with words like *samsara* and *nirvana, kinhin* and *gassho.* Two words in particular—*dukkha* and *dharma*—evoked more questions than they answered.

Dukkha is most often translated into English as "suffering." But the original Pali term carries a broader definition, describing the full spectrum of human difficulty and distress, from mild irritation or annoyance to full-throttle grief, rage, or madness. Alternate translations include "angst," "stress," "unsatisfactoriness," and my personal favorite: "a wheel out of round."

Dukkha includes the inevitable pain and affliction that come with living in a body, the rub of having to be around unpleasant people or in annoying situations, the ache of being separated from friends and loved ones, and the frustration that no matter how smart we are or how hard we work to manage and control our circumstances, things keep shifting and changing.

The existential truth of *dukkha* is understood in Buddhism as the doorway to spiritual practice. In some accounts, the Buddha is reputed to have summed up his entire teaching in one phrase: "I teach one thing and one thing only: suffering and the end of suffering."

Now here was a teaching I could relate to.

I understood the truth of suffering. But when I was growing up, to speak directly about suffering was taboo in my family. To admit feeling pain—or even worse, to complain about it—was an embarrassment, an admission of failure. The fact that the people at the Zen center spoke often and openly about *dukkha* was a profound relief to me.

The meaning of the second word, *dharma,* was more perplexing. It was a term I heard often but couldn't grasp. Sometimes dharma was described as the Buddha's teaching, sometimes as the cosmic law of the universe, sometimes simply as the truth. Before classes and lectures at the Zen center we would chant: *Dharma gates are boundless, I vow to enter them.* I didn't know what a "dharma gate" was. But the more I sat and bowed and chanted, the more I wanted to step across the threshold.

I learned more about the meaning of dharma one Saturday when I went to the Zen center to hear a talk by a visiting Japanese teacher named Kobun-chino. I took my seat in the Buddha Hall and watched as Kobun entered the room, a wisp of a man with a warm, gentle demeanor and a cloudlike gait. He stopped and bowed to a life-size statue on one side of the altar. We all watched as he gazed at the statue, his palms raised, leaning in, as if they were having an intimate conversation. Then he settled into his seat and slowly, haltingly, began to speak. His voice was thin and raspy, more breath than sound. As he spoke, the entire room fell silent, trying to catch every word.

When the bell sounded and the talk was over, I scurried into the dining room where Kobun would be taking questions. I took a seat in the front row and waited.

Kobun sat on a couch with his legs crossed, carefully gathering and tucking his robes under him. Someone had placed a celadon tea set on the coffee table in front of him. He leaned over and poured a cup of tea, the scent of jasmine filling the room. He lifted the cup with two hands, brought the cup to his lips, took a slow sip, and then set the cup back down on the table. He paused and then looked up across the room.

"Any questions?" he asked.

No one said anything. People sat with their eyes closed or looking down at their feet.

My hand shot up. I didn't know then that my unreserved enthusiasm was not customary. I was still new to Zen culture and finding my way. But I was certain Kobun could tell me what I wanted to know.

He turned to face me. "Yes?"

I said, "What is . . . the dharma?"

A wave of laughter rolled through the room. Even Kobun chuckled.

"I don't know," he said, drawing out each syllable.

I pressed forward, undaunted. "No, really," I persisted. "I'm new here. I keep hearing the word 'dharma' and I don't know what it means."

Kobun paused. He pressed his lips together in a soft pucker and took in my words. The room fell quiet. He waited. I waited. And then he did something that has stayed with me all these years.

He leaned over, picked up the teapot, and held it up in front of him. Then he looked at me and said: "The dharma . . . the dharma is what holds this teapot together." Then he placed the teapot back on the table.

I had no idea what he was talking about. But something about what he said went right in. His words rang inside me like something forgotten—something I couldn't name but knew was true.

He hooked me. What holds a teapot together? I would do anything to find the answer.

As spring tipped toward summer, a flow of new Zen students began arriving and departing for Tassajara, a storied mountain monastery nestled deep in California's Ventana Wilderness. Closed to the general public for intensive monastic training in the rainy fall and icy winter, the monastery opened for the guest season during the summer months.

One morning I had a conversation about Tassajara with Paul, one of the head teachers at the Zen center. Paul was an imposing figure, tall and lean, with a craggy face and an Irish brogue. When he took in questions, he would tilt his head to the right, occasionally lifting an eyebrow to indicate curiosity or surprise.

I was sitting at the breakfast table when Paul scooted into the seat across from me. My once-warm bowl of oatmeal, stewed fruit, and sesame salt sat between us. I looked up with a tentative smile.

"Good morning," he said, placing his palms together and making a small bow. A prolonged pause unfolded. I kept my eyes cast down. Paul clasped his hands on the table in front of him and leaned in. "So when are *you* going to Tassajara?" he asked.

I spilled the full length of my sad story to him: how the trip to China fell through, how I'd ended up in a dreary job, and how I wanted to quit but felt stuck. I even told him about the nightmare of the rat and my battle with my body. He took in my words with a quality of tenderness that allowed me to feel the full weight of my unhappiness. Yes, I wanted to go to the monastery. But I was afraid to say I wanted it out loud. I didn't want to be that vulnerable or to face the possibility of more rejection. I blotted my eyes with my crumpled napkin and held my breath.

"Of course you can go to Tassajara," Paul said. "Follow me." I walked with him down the wide hallway, listening to the swish of his robes, and watching the red linoleum pass under our feet. Paul stopped at the front office and greeted the woman behind the desk with a short bow. "Pam would like an application to Tassajara," he told her.

Six weeks later I was on my way.

2

AWAKENING WONDER

In 1967 Shunryu Suzuki Roshi established Tassajara as the first Zen monastery on Western soil, tucked away in a narrow valley in the Santa Lucia Mountains in central California. Off the grid and barely on the map, with only a single old-fashioned crank telephone, the monastery was insulated from the world by steep mountains dense with chaparral and manzanita.

It took more than an hour to traverse the seventeen-mile dirt road leading to Tassajara, bumping across washboards and deep, tire-spinning ruts. With each mile, the familiar world of cement, speed, telephones, electricity, and fossil-fueled ambition slipped further away. I had traded in my colorful skirts and scarves for simple black robes, T-shirts, jeans, work boots, and clogs. There would be no more calling up my friends or ambling down the street to the local supermarket or café.

Six of us were packed into a rugged four-wheel-drive vehicle affectionately called the "stage" in memory of the horse-and-buggy jaunts travelers took in the late 1800s when journeying over the Santa Lucia mountains to Tassajara's natural hot springs. In those days, the final downhill stretch of the road was so steep that a twenty-foot-long tree trunk had to be chained to the stagecoach's rear axles to keep the coach from careening into the horses on the steep downgrade.

We pressed our faces against the stage's windows, drinking in the untamed beauty of the landscape. Conversations sparked up—*What's your name? Where are you from? How long will you be staying?*—and sputtered back into silence as we bumped along, our eagerness tempered by the sound of scraping tires, thick clouds of dust, and mild nausea.

I had spent the prior several weeks in a flurry of activity: I quit my job, packed up my apartment, canceled my phone service, and buzz-cut my dark Medusa curls to half an inch of stubble. My belly fluttered and my mind spun every time I imagined passing through the monastery gates, stepping across the threshold from the life I had known into a simpler time and place.

As we pulled into the parking lot, Keith, our stage driver, whose round face and deep-set eyes were etched with smile lines, turned and offered a hearty welcome. "Getting over the road is the hard part," he said with a twinkling grin. "Welcome to Tassajara." We clicked open the doors, peeled our bodies out of the air-conditioned seats, and stood in the hot sun, shaking out the kinks in our limbs while Keith slid out of the driver's seat, brushed an inch of red dust off the back doors of the van, and pulled out our bags.

I dumped my overstuffed duffle bags into a creaky wooden cart with fat tires, and I towed the cart from the parking lot across stone and dirt pathways to my new home: a narrow room with just enough space for a futon mattress and a rickety chair, with a few hooks poking out from the back of the door and five bent hangers dangling from a wooden beam. The single window at the foot of the bed was lined with thick, clear plastic rather than glass. Cracks in the walls leaked grit from outside.

I dragged my bags into the room, stacked them in the corner, flung myself onto the lumpy bed, and stared up at the uneven ceiling, grinning.

As a summer work-practice student, I received room and board in exchange for working to support the monastery's four-month guest season, catering to travelers who signed up to enjoy rustic cabins, gourmet vegetarian food, and steaming sulfur baths. My stay at Tassajara was like summer camp for adults: physical labor, clear skies, cool water, warm friendships, mosquitos, the smell of fresh-baked bread wafting up from the kitchen, and sonorous chanting instead of campfire songs.

I spent my first several months chopping vegetables, clearing tables, and learning to turn fresh sheets of emptied guest beds with crisp hospital corners. I sat silently in the meditation hall each morning and evening, and I sat at outdoor picnic tables with new students and grizzled, cheerful longtime monks over platefuls of hearty food.

As the summer season rolled to a close, I was reluctant to drive back over the mountain and reenter the "real" world. I had been admitted to graduate school at UC Berkeley in public health beginning that fall, but when the welcome packet arrived I could barely read it. "Social Policy 101" sounded bleak in contrast to the intellectual inspiration I found in the writings of thirteenth-century Zen master Dogen Zenji; the emotional welcome I felt as the warm arms of the community took me in; and the sense of physical ease (and blood sugar stability) that unfolded in me as I settled into a consistent daily schedule, with three wholesome meals a day.

When the last summer guests left, the tiny hamlet of Tassajara quieted. We spent a month preparing for the onset of winter and the intimate silence of monastic training. I drafted a letter to Berkeley deferring my enrollment and took a trip into town to purchase long underwear, wool socks, and slip-on rain shoes in preparation for the turn of the seasons. I wrote cards to my friends and family to tell them: *I am not coming home.*

I had imagined monastic practice would be esoteric and profound. I was surprised to discover how simple it was: wake up, sit in meditation, bow and chant, eat, study, work, bathe, repeat. I was assigned to the general maintenance crew for three hours of work each afternoon: moving piles of rocks, chopping wood, pulling weeds. After work and tea, there was a break for bath time in the sulfur tubs, pools of warmth set beneath looming sandstone mountain walls. I stripped, sliding naked into the thermal springs piped in from the creek, easing out the ache of long hours sitting upright in meditation. As the late afternoon light softened and evening crept in, the rich sound of the bell rang through the valley, calling us back for evening bowing and chanting.

Each day began at 3:30 a.m. with the clanging of the wake-up bell. The first thing I did was to pull a smoky glass globe off of the kerosene lamp on my night table and light the wick, creating a pool of golden light. It was bitter cold, and I did not want to crawl out from under my down comforter into the sharp air. But each day I rolled out of bed, wearing thick long johns, and scurried to the toilet. I would perch above the seat, straining to keep the icy surface from touching my warm skin. Then I wrapped myself in long black robes, covered my buzz cut with a wool cap, blew out the lamp, and headed out.

In the early morning before daybreak, the sky was a symphony of stars. A steady stream of dark-robed bodies shuffled toward the meditation hall, exhaling white puffs of breath. I climbed the stairs, kicked off my clogs, peeled off my socks and placed them on the shoe rack outside the meditation hall, and then tiptoed along the chilly wooden walkway to the door. Before entering the *zendo* (the monastery's meditation hall), I placed my palms together in *gassho*, stepped over the threshold, and made a small bow.

I bowed again toward and away from my seat, and then hoisted myself onto my round *zafu* (meditation cushion), folding my legs under me, leaning left and then right, and settling into a relaxed, upright spine. Sixty of us sat together, shoulder to shoulder, a line of breathing bodies. Minutes unfolded in fluid time. As the darkness lifted, the sound of birds chirping floated through the shoji-screen windows, and the gentle tapping of the drum and bell signaled the opening of a new day.

After a few weeks of consistent sleepiness, I began to settle in and find a rhythm. Long stretches of silence were punctuated by bursts of sound: the clang of the wake-up bell, the *whoosh* of a wooden match igniting a kerosene lamp, the rustle of robes, the squawking of the jays, the brisk *tok tok tok* of the thick wooden block, struck with a mallet, to summon us to meditation.

"The schedule is like putting a snake in a bamboo pole," one of my teachers explained. "A snake is curvy. The pole is straight." I assumed she meant straight is good and curvy is bad, but that wasn't what she meant at all. Being contained within the tight circle of the monastic schedule revealed my unique curves, quirks, and preferences. Deeply held beliefs and opinions were laid bare. I discovered expectations I hadn't known I was carrying.

I'd arrived wanting quiet, spaciousness, peace. Instead, my mind spun like a fiery pinwheel, shooting sparks in all directions. I was flooded with petty judgments, fear, and longing. And I could barely contain my disappointment.

"I thought once I got to the monastery everything would quiet down," I confessed to my teacher. "But all this stillness just makes the inner ruckus even louder."

She smiled. "It's not about stopping the ruckus," she explained. "Our practice is not about transcendence. It's about getting to know all the parts of ourselves, especially those we have ignored or abandoned."

"Can I go home now?" I asked, half-joking.

I had imagined that after a few months of deep meditation practice, I'd be done: all my bad behaviors and unseemly habits would be uprooted. Instead, they came out in full force, a colorful parade of ugliness and pain, fueling relentless self-criticism and doubt.

"It's a slow, humbling process of meeting the places we don't like and learning to hold them with patience and with kindness," the teacher continued.

This is not what I signed up for, I thought. But I knew she was right. While the content of my experience was wearisome and annoying, I could see that learning to be with it, hour after hour, day after day, was having an impact. I was softer, less defended, more open. Even brimming with inner judgment and self-reproach, I had to admit: I liked who I was becoming.

I was happy to learn that before the Buddha became enlightened, he struggled, too. One story describes how, as he sat beneath the Bo tree, silent and resolute, the soon-to-be-Buddha was assailed by the armies of Mara. In Buddhist mythology, Mara is a kind of demon. He can also be understood as an archetype, the personification of what we might call the superego or the inner critic: those primitive energies that erupt in us as inner voices that cajole or condemn. Mara's aim is to keep us safe and the *same*—to avoid danger and maintain homeostasis.

Because enlightenment involves a radical shift, upending everything familiar and constant, Mara shows up repeatedly in the stories of the Buddha, nagging and taunting him. Buddhist texts describe Mara pummeling the ardent young seeker with arrows as he sits in deep meditation. As each arrow comes his way, Siddhartha Gotama (as the Buddha was named at birth) uses the power of mindfulness to become aware of what is happening and calls out, "I see you, Mara." Each time Mara is seen and named, his arrow-taunts and insults transform in midair into lotus blossoms that burst open, showering Siddhartha with fragrant petals. When we see things as they are and name them, they lose their sting.

But Mara is persistent. When his arrows fail, he puts down his bow, sidles up to Siddhartha, hovers over his shoulder, and whispers in his ear: *Who do you think you are?*

This question goes right to the heart of the spiritual journey. Who are we? But Mara's tone is not curious or benevolent. His question is spoken with derision, more demand than true inquiry. He is challenging Siddhartha's self-worth. And remember, in this story Siddhartha is not the Buddha yet. He is an ex-prince and ex-ascetic, a solitary seeker, ostracized by his friends, stripped of his exalted identities. He is vulnerable and alone.

In response to Mara's question, Siddhartha does not declare or defend. Instead he makes a simple gesture: he reaches down and touches the earth, expressing his unshakable confidence. "The earth herself is my witness," he declares. I am here. I belong.

Earth; humus; humility. The gesture of touching the earth encourages us to look down, not up, and to feel the support of the ground beneath us. As I slowly learned to navigate my own voices of doubt and unworthiness, I felt the ground grow solid beneath me. As I learned to drop into the immediacy of my own physical experience and embody the earthiness of my own flesh, bit by bit, I began to discover: *I, too, belong.*

After several months, the hum and churn inside me began to subside. As my body softened, I discovered a visceral stability and poise I didn't know was possible. I rolled back my daily insulin until I was taking half my normal dose. The familiar mental cacophony of commentary and comparison, worry and distrust, softened. While my inner chatter remained, it became more of a background murmur, soft echoes that rose and fell as if heard down a long hallway.

One morning in the cool dark before daybreak, I noticed something was different. It was the sound of the creek. The quiet rush of water had transformed overnight from a burble to a roar. I was perplexed: what had caused the creek to shift?

During afternoon tea, I recounted my observation to one of the old-timers, a tall, stooped man with graying stubble and flyaway eyebrows who had passed thirteen winters as a monk. His broad smile revealed yellowing teeth as he signaled me to sit with him on the stoop outside his cabin. Reaching into the long sleeve of his fraying robe, he pulled out a package of Drum tobacco and rolled a skinny cigarette.

"What happened to the creek?" I asked him.

"It's the sycamores," he told me, pointing to the canopy of green above us, formed by grand trees with mottled bark and wooly leaves that line the pathways of Tassajara. "As winter approaches, they gather water in their roots and trunks. When the temperature drops, all that stored water is released into the water table, causing the creek to rise."

He paused.

"You'll see," he continued. "Over the next days the sycamore leaves will begin to change color and fall."

Sure enough, over the next few days I watched as the sycamore leaves turned shades of gold, ginger, and brown. They began tumbling from the gnarled branches of the trees, blanketing the earth with a quilt of color, filling me with a long-forgotten sense of wonder and awe.

How did they know? How did all the sycamores know to drop their water at the *same time?* What secret language did they share? I imagined some ethereal orchestra conductor hiding in the hills who waved his baton, declaring: *one, two, three . . . okay, everybody drop!*

In his book *The Hidden Life of Trees* ecologist Peter Wohlleben describes the forest as a vibrant community brimming with complex, intricate communication. Trees, it turns out, talk among themselves. They converse in their own inscrutable language. A community of trees shares nutrients with the aged and ailing among it, and it warns its members of impending danger, Wohlleben explains. There are many scientific hypotheses for how this happens—capillary action, transpiration, osmosis, temperature. But none of them fully explain the phenomenon. The truth is, we don't fully understand how it works, Wohlleben insists. "Perhaps we are poorer for having lost an explanation," he muses, "or richer for having gained a mystery."

But of course, as Flannery O'Connor memorably noted, "Mystery is a great embarrassment to the modern mind." I had grown up in a family and culture that prized intellectual knowledge, and I'd spent years honing my capacity to discriminate and discern. Not knowing the answer to a question was cause for shame.

But not-knowing is highly prized in Zen. As my spiritual practice deepened, I learned to embrace mystery as the living, pulsing heartbeat of the path. At Tassajara, I began to sink my roots into the earth and twine my limbs with the trees while the creek, the jays, and the sky reawakened the wide-eyed child in me.

I first met Bodhidharma at Tassajara one evening when I was seated in the woodstove-warmed community dining room, poring over an inscrutable text by Dogen-zenji, the thirteenth-century Japanese philosopher-poet-monk. Bodhidharma's image was staring down at me from a sumi ink scroll on the wall behind me. When I pushed my chair back, I accidentally bumped the scroll, which came tumbling off the wall and landed with a thud on the table in front of me.

There he was, one of the central characters in Zen lore, responsible for bringing Buddhism from India over the mountains into China, looking up at me. Bodhidharma's nickname is the "red-haired barbarian," referring to his unusually tall stature and heavy, red beard. As I looked down at him, he glared back, with his bulging eyes, bushy eyebrows and thick gold hoop earrings descending from long, droopy lobes—a fierce, imposing figure with a grumpy countenance that made him look as if he had indigestion.

The legend of Bodhidharma tells that he cut off his eyelids to prevent himself from falling asleep in meditation. As he tossed his eyelids onto the ground, they turned into seeds that grew to become the green tea plants used by Buddhist monks in China to keep themselves from falling asleep during long hours sitting in meditation.

Bodhidharma was a renegade and a rebel. When he arrived in China, the emperor, who was a scholarly, devout Buddhist, invited him to come to the palace for a visit. When Bodhidharma arrived, the emperor asked him, "What is the highest meaning of the holy truths?"

Bodhidharma, who was neither devout nor holy, answered brusquely, "Emptiness, nothing holy," and turned to take his leave.

"Emptiness" is an English translation of the Sanskrit term *sunyata*, one of the most misunderstood terms in the Buddhist lexicon. *Emptiness* does not mean *nothingness*. It is not a terrifying, nihilistic void. It is an invitation to true intimacy. According to Bodhidharma, the highest truths are not esoteric or holy; they are always standing right here in front of us. *Come closer,* the teachings on emptiness whisper, *keep looking, and then look some more.*

"Wait!" the emperor called out. "Who are you standing before me?" His question mirrored Mara's question to Siddhartha, but with a tone of respect and reverence.

"I don't know," Bodhidharma replied.

Bodhidharma's "I don't know" has echoed down through the ages. In Chinese, the word *sunyata* is translated with the character for "sky." Bodhidharma's emptiness and not-knowing point toward a skylike awareness: open, spacious, shot through with the willingness to tolerate ambiguity and the courage not to know.

Each morning, after several hours of silent meditation, the community chanted the Heart Sutra, an abbreviated version of the ancient Perfection of Wisdom or *Prajnaparamita* Sutra. One day we would chant it in Japanese, the next day in English. "Avalokitesvara Bodhisattva," we called out into the brightening morning, "when deeply practicing perceived that all five *skandhas* are empty and thus relieved all suffering."

The Sanskrit word *skandha* means "heap" or "aggregate." It describes the five components that comprise a moment of sensory experience: *rupa*—physical forms, including the body; *vedana*—the pleasant, unpleasant, and neutral feelings and sensations that arise as we interact with forms; *samjna*—discrimination and conceptualization, which include labeling or naming; *samskara*—our historical habits, assumptions, and biases that inform how we relate to each experience; and *vijnana*—the sensory consciousness that arises with each moment.

Let's take a simple example of how this works: seeing a red apple. When this happens, form (an apple) and consciousness (seeing) meet. The red blob sitting on the table registers as pleasant ("yum"), unpleasant ("yuck), or neutral ("uninteresting"). Quickly after it registers, we name it ("oh, an apple"). Our present experience of "apple" is shaped by our past experience: "My mother used to give us apples as a special treat," or, "The last apple I ate had a worm in it." Based on this, we either reach for the apple and take a bite, or we grimace and turn away.

In Buddhist iconography, Avalokitesvara Bodhisattva is depicted as having eleven heads and a thousand arms, a halo of limbs reaching out in all directions to "hear the cries of the world." The Japanese figure of Avalokitesvara represents the archetype of kindness, compassion, mercy, and love, represented across spiritual traditions in different forms: Mother Mary in Christianity, Tara in Tibet, Quan Yin in China.

In the opening line of the Heart Sutra, Avalokitesvara, the Bodhisattva of Great Compassion, sees that the five *skandhas*—these fundamental building blocks of our experience—are "empty"; they do not exist as separate, solid, permanent entities. Like Bodhidharma's "empty, nothing holy," the Heart Sutra suggests that the realization of emptiness "relieves all suffering."

Buddhist teaching uses the metaphor of a bird to describe the two wings needed to engage the spiritual path: one wing is wisdom—clearly seeing into the emptiness of all things; and the other wing is compassion—the ability to bring care and kindness to everything we see. Both wings are needed to fly.

When I arrived at Tassajara, my wings were battered and askew. A few nights before making the journey over the long road to Tassajara, I had a going-away dinner with a circle of friends. After consuming sesame noodles and garlic shrimp, I cracked open my fortune cookie, which read: "Knowledge is learning something every day. Wisdom is letting go of something every day."

I knew how to gather knowledge. I loved learning. But I was not very wise. Wisdom was daunting: it demanded letting go, stepping into the unknown. I knew how to think, and I knew how to try hard, but I knew very little about surrender.

Each day as I chanted the words of the sutra, I felt a longing to understand emptiness. My idea of emptiness was that it would empty me of all my pain so I could transcend, floating happily above the density and trouble of my body. I wanted emptiness to gut me, leaving me clean, pristine, and untroubled.

In my familiar, zealous, hardworking way, I took up a practice I called "putting others first." Every day I made an effort to notice and contain my pushy habit of getting ahead. I let others ask questions, step in front of me to gather morning tea, take the last scoop of spinach salad or lasagna from the bowl or pan. Who could argue with that? It felt so pure and virtuous.

I proudly told one of the senior teachers about my new effort. "I've been doing a compassion practice of putting others first," I said.

I waited for praise, for confirmation of my selfless virtue. He said nothing.

Undaunted, I continued: "I'm practicing putting others first so that my false sense of solid self will soften. I'm practicing compassion to help me wake up."

There was a long, uncomfortable silence.

Finally, he spoke. "Someday you will understand," he said slowly, "that you have it exactly backwards."

A flash of irritation bristled through me. *He doesn't understand,* I thought. But I was the one who didn't get it.

I was proud of my intelligence, but I easily missed the forest for the trees. And if my wisdom wing was tattered, my compassion wing was completely broken. I knew little about how to hold myself with kindness or to extend gentleness and empathy to others.

Over the next weeks, I kept chewing on the teacher's words, replaying the scene in my mind. Part of me continued to feel annoyed and misunderstood. But something about what he said stuck in me. What was it I didn't understand?

Then one morning while chanting the Heart Sutra, the words of the sutra's opening line did a somersault in my mind. It was as if someone had tossed them up into the air, and when they landed, I heard them in an entirely new way.

"Avalokitesvara Bodhisattva when deeply practicing perceived that all five *skandhas* are empty and thus relieved all suffering."

Oh! I realized I had been paying attention to the wrong thing. It is Avalokitesvara, the bodhisattva of compassion, who wakes up. Awakening to empty *skandhas* was not the point. The whole point of the sutra was the awakening of *compassion.*

To my chagrin, I saw that my seemingly altruistic practice of putting others first was actually ambitious and transactional. I had been using compassion as a means to an end. I had been engaging in a compassion practice in order to cultivate wisdom. But that morning I began to understand: the culmination of the path is not awakening; it is living a life of compassion.

When Dogen-zenji was approaching his death, he called his beloved disciple Tetsu Gikai to his deathbed. Tetsu was a highly capable, impeccable student, primed to become Dogen's successor. "You understand all of Buddhism," Dogen told him, "but your abilities and your intelligence are not enough. You must go beyond your intellect and understanding and cultivate *robai-shin*, the mind of great compassion for helping all of humanity, not just yourself."

Robai-shin means "grandmotherly mind," the ability to hear and see and hold others with sympathetic, sensitive hands. When I was young, it was my mother's mother, Helen, who taught me about this. Grandma Helen was a short, feisty Jew from the old country with square shoulders and persistent indigestion. Her sentences were punctuated by small gasps and burps. She smelled of baby powder and lemon drops. She was my advocate and cheerleader.

She would arrive at our home in California in a tailored wool suit, stockings, and leather gloves, with one of her many rhinestone insect brooches pinned to her lapel: green dragonflies, orange monarchs, black-spotted ladybugs, shimmering spiders. After retiring briefly to her room, she'd reappear in a simple cotton housedress, her stockings rolled down around her ankles, polished pumps traded for puffy, padded slippers.

Cinching an apron around her waist, Helen commandeered the kitchen, churning out pots of beef tongue, trays of apricot kugel, and platters of chocolate-drizzled toffee squares, meringue cookies, and coffee cake. We called her the "goodie grandma." As she worked her magic in the kitchen, I sat perched on the countertop, watching her soft, strong hands knead, salt, slice, and stir.

"*Nu, bubelah?*" she would ask, walking over to pinch my cheek between her puffy fingers. "How are you? Tell me everything."

And so I did. Helen listened as I prattled on, absorbing my childhood stories: the fight I had with my friend Marcy, the red-haired boy on the bus who pulled my hair, how my pet guinea pig, Nibbles, gave birth to six tiny albino babies. Her listening was nourishment, cool water on parched soil. As she listened, I bloomed.

The power of listening is depicted in a story about George Washington Carver, the brilliant botanist and social reformer whose devotion to the natural world helped revolutionize farming practices in the South. Born in Missouri in 1864 to enslaved parents, he was a sickly child whose physical frailty prevented him from working in the fields. But even as a child, his green thumb was legendary, and he was nicknamed "the little plant doctor." The women in young George's community would bring their ailing plants to him, and he would take them to the plant hospital he'd created in the woods behind his cabin and nurse them back to life.

One day an elderly woman came to collect her once-ailing, now-thriving houseplant. She asked him, "Little George, what is your secret? How do you heal all these dying plants?"

With the wisdom of an ageless Zen master, he replied, "If you listen to things and love them, they will reveal themselves to you."

Listening and loving. This is the essence of grandmotherly mind. When we meet the world with our ears and eyes and hearts and hands wide open, it opens, too, revealing its secrets. Like Grandma Helen and little George, I was learning to listen with love.

A few weeks after my early-morning revelation about Avalokitesvara and awakening compassion, I had a dream: I was walking through the countryside—rolling green hills, blue sky, sunshine, and picket fences. In the distance I saw a house with a woman standing on the broad porch, signaling me to come in. I climbed the steps and entered. In silence, she led me into the kitchen. On the floor there was a wicker basket full of puppies, six fluffy balls of unrestrained glee.

I understood that I was supposed to select *my* puppy to take home with me. I crouched down, picking up each puppy, snuggling and smiling as they squirmed and licked my face. I raised each one above my head, peering into its face, until I found the one I knew was mine. I stood and held him aloft, and we gazed into each other's eyes with delight.

Suddenly, the puppy sprouted fangs. His tiny face grimaced, and he began to snarl. I startled, almost dropping him, but a quiet voice inside me said: *Don't flinch. The puppy is scared. Hold him steady.*

As he growled, I continued to hold him in my hands. I cooed gently, humming. Little by little, his face began to soften. I bent my arms, bringing his face close to my face. As I did, he began to transform from a fluffy puppy into a tender, pink baby. I looked into his eyes and pulled him closer still, cradling him into my chest. We stood together rocking, nested, skin to skin.

When I woke from the dream, I understood. This is what it means to listen with love. This is how to reach down and touch the earth. Stay rooted and open. Coo and hum. Don't flinch. Hold the puppy. Hold the puppy. Hold the puppy.

3

I WANT TO BE FREE

The long shadow of the Holocaust spilled through the sunny hallways of my childhood home. Lining the walls of the stairwell that led upstairs was a series of photographs. My ancestors, poised, stared out from behind the glass in rich sepia tones: men in topcoats, starched shirts, and polished shoes; women in long belted skirts and pressed blouses; little boys in shorts, and little girls with wide white bows in their hair.

My mother would tap the glass with her long nails as she ushered me upstairs to bed at night. "He survived and he survived and she survived," she said. "The rest of them burned in the ovens." For years I tucked away the images in those photographs, holding them at arm's length as alien, as other. I refused to swallow the knowledge of that impossible human cruelty.

There is an image used to describe the process of meditation: Imagine a glass jar filled with water and dirt. If you place a lid on the jar and shake it, what do you get? Muddy water. This murky brew is the chop, churn, and swirl of the mind, tossed about by the tempests of everyday life.

Now, if you set the jar down, what happens? Bit by bit, the silt settles to the bottom, eventually revealing pristine, clear water.

That's how meditation works. First there is stopping: slowing down and pausing long enough to let the waters calm and the dirt sink to the bottom. Then there is clear seeing: insights that arise in unsoiled water. Settling down and waking up go hand in hand. It's a circular process, slowly allowing us to unhook from habitual patterns and opening possibilities for engaging life in new ways.

But there is more. Once the dirt settles and the water clears, stuff bubbles up from the bottom: raw, undigested memories, unfinished business, fear, trauma. Cast-off pieces of our past, lurking in muscle memory, resurface and cry out. It's a process of re-membering. *Member* means "part," and *re-* means "again." To re-member is to stitch the forgotten pieces back together again, metabolize what is undigested, and weave life back into wholeness.

After a few months at Tassajara, the bubbling up began for me. I had become a placid lake, cool and collected. Then a deep tremor arose that swept through my body. There were no words or images, just wave upon wave of sadness. For days I wept. Tears spilled down my cheeks, leaving the crisp white collar of my under robe salty and wet. I had come for the beauty, quiet, and peace, but as I softened into the arms of the community, I was swept by a fierce flood of sorrow.

I was wary of sharing my sadness. For years I had been told to tuck my unhappiness out of sight. Now, as uncomfortable as it was to feel my sadness, I did not want to stop. My tears were awkward and unpleasant, but they also brought great relief.

No one suggested I stop. Instead, they passed the tissues and offered ample space for my wordless grief to flow and unfold.

One morning I was startled out of a deep slumber. Lying in the dark, in the liminal space between sleeping and waking, I saw them: the women in the photographs, huddled, their dark eyes and sharp cheekbones heightened by hunger. I watched their frail bodies, stooped and bent, waiting in line, clutching bars of soap in their bony hands. I saw how they offered each other moments of solace with a whisper, a gaze, a touch.

I squeezed my eyes shut and rolled over, wishing them away. But they refused to go, hovering around me like shadows. *We live in you,* they whispered: as the hardening of your skin; as your habit of pulling inward; as all the things you never say; as the way you retreat into the warmth of your imagination. We did that, too, they tell me. We, too, unfastened sorrow from our tired bones and descended into darkness. As relief, as reprieve. But you know this, too, they said: the yearning to be released from the bitterness of the body.

I watched as they twisted and crouched, pressed into cold cement chambers, frightened and weary. I listened as they inhaled gas, gasping. I felt their lungs seize. But before they passed, I heard their final invocation and blessing. What we want you to know, they told me, is this: *we did not want to die.*

Their unequivocal "yes" echoed inside me bittersweetly—a clear call to release the burden of disappointment I carried in my pockets like stones. Their words silenced my own ambivalence toward life. I received those words as a promise, but also as a fierce demand: Uncross your arms. Stop pounding on other people's doors. Throw open the windows. Step into your life.

For decades I had dreamed of dying. Throughout adolescence it was the same dream: tumbling through space, arms and legs flailing, then waking with a start into the hushed night, heart pounding, limbs trembling, damp with perspiration. In later years, the rush toward death in dreams came in different ways: as a volley of bullets; the sharp slicing of metal through skin; gasping and sputtering for breath in a churning sea; the scent of searing flesh as I burned at the stake. I would feel myself rushing down a dark tunnel toward the light, but just before I entered, I would startle awake.

After the early-morning Holocaust visitation at Tassajara, a new image arose during my meditation. Again and again I would feel myself pulled toward a cool, black lake. As I sat and my mind and body softened, I would feel my edges blur and become fluid, like water. My amorphous water-body would be magnetically drawn toward the edge of a pool of darkness.

At first I stopped at the shore, pulling back. But over time, first a foot, then a leg, then both legs were absorbed into the inky, black waters. One day I found myself up to my neck. Another day, the full length of me was floating in the lake on my back, staring up at the sparkling night sky. Then, just like in the falling dreams of my adolescence, I would gasp and startle, my eyes would snap open, and I would land back in the meditation hall, my hands clammy, my heart pounding.

This was not about seeing into crisp, clear waters. It was about being submerged in darkness and mud. All the rigid formality of Zen—the tight container of the schedule, the proper foot to use to step over the threshold of the zendo, the meticulous attention to posture and detail—provided a firm, stable latticework that allowed the long-buried fear and inner chaos of my heart-mind to be revealed and released.

I never told anyone about the dark lake. It felt too intimate and strange. But I brought what I learned in meditation to the experience: stay close; be curious and kind; pay attention to your *relationship* to what is happening as much as to the content of the experience. What I discovered was a surprise. Just under the surface of terror was a tender ache—the deep yearning to be absorbed into that black pool of stillness.

This realization brought new layers of dread. Did I want to die? It was easy to confuse my mother's suicidal inclinations for my own. I was not the only one in my family sheltering secrets. My mother, with her high-pitched giggle and strong potter's hands, quietly suffered the travails of bipolar disorder. Over the years there were handfuls of sleeping pills, episodes of stomach pumping, hospitalizations, electric shock treatments. None of this was ever discussed out loud, but it lived as an unexpressed torque in the family system, a vague discomfort I could feel but never quite name. It was a secret that inhabited my body as a twist in my ribcage and a curling forward of my shoulders to protect my heart. It played out in my relationships with others as the cool, gray shield I slipped behind to deflect the threat of kindness or intimacy.

It took care and precision to slowly untangle the threads of my mother's psyche that were entangled with mine. Bit by bit I came to understand that her manic crescendos and steep, gloomy descents were rife with torment and that she was ambivalent about being alive.

As the months passed and I deepened my capacity to be still and listen, I came to understand that the tremors, tears, dreams, and visions that tormented my tranquility were not the same as my mother's death wish. Yes, there was a deep pull toward letting go, dissolving, coming undone. But I did not want to die. I wanted to be free.

4

FREEDOM IS POSSIBLE

I am seated at a picnic table in a garden. It is a sparkling blue day. Cool, green grass. The scent of eucalyptus. Leaves rustling in the ocean breeze. The remainders of a picnic are scattered across the table's rough planks: a half-eaten baguette, an assortment of cheeses, roast chicken and rice, plump strawberries. A man in a baseball cap is tossing a Frisbee to his son. A woman lies stretched across the picnic bench, soaking up the warm rays of the sun.

A man rushes up with a red face and furrowed brow. He is out of breath. We are in the path of a giant tsunami, he tells us. A towering wall of water is rumbling toward the coastline. It will arrive any minute. I understand: this is it, the end of the world. In a matter of moments everyone and everything will be swept away by a massive rush of water.

The earth trembles. The ground beneath us shakes and rattles. I look up. The sky is swirling. Day and night twist and blur. Sunlight shines. Clouds pass. Stars twinkle. Past, present, and future unfurl simultaneously as a singular moment of time.

I stand awed, overcome by the raw beauty of what is unfolding. My heart aches for the web of relationships surrounding me that, in a few short moments, will all be gone.

The wave hits. I grip the side of the table with clenched hands, trying to hang on as I inhale salt water and am swept into a churning amniotic sea. There is a moment of sheer panic. Then I hear a quiet, steady voice in my head whisper: *Just let go.* To let go means I will die. I don't want to die. But I can't hold on any longer.

I release my grip and fall back into the rush of water. Stillness descends. I am filled with the most exquisite contentment, ease, and quiet delight.

My eyes fluttered open, and I stared into the blackness of my room at Tassajara. I lay perfectly still. I did not want to break the spell of the dream. I wanted the feeling of pure serenity and bliss to last and last. For a few moments after, there was no fear and no doubt. The anxious reverberation in my nervous system fell away. I was infused with wordless understanding: Oh, this is how it feels to be released.

After his enlightenment, the Buddha was strolling along, enjoying his peace and contentment. A wanderer saw him and was struck by his radiance and serene demeanor.

"Who are you?" the wanderer asked. "Some kind of *deva* or celestial being?"

"No," the Buddha replied, "I am not a god."

"Then what are you?"

"I am awake."

What does it mean to awaken? The possibility of awakening is the premise and promise of the Buddhist path. "It is possible," the Buddha is reputed to have told his monks. "If it were not possible, I would not ask you to do it." But what he describes as "possible" is not a state of eternal bliss. It is an ongoing, unfolding process of understanding and embodying truth and love.

What the seeker Siddhartha Gotama discovered was not a magic pill or secret sauce. It was a process of waking up to the fullness of our potential as human beings by seeing through the obstacles that bind and blind us. What Siddhartha learned after years of concentrated effort was that human suffering is not the result of evil, but of ignorance. Our suffering is born of confusion. It is, fundamentally, a case of mistaken identity.

We mistake ourselves as being some *thing*. But, according to a Buddhist teaching, who we are is not a *thing* at all. This is the teaching of *anatta:* there is no separate, solid self. What the Buddha came to see is that who we are is an ever-changing stream of experience. And when we cling—to our firmly held ideas, beliefs, roles, and identities—we freeze-frame reality, turning flowing water into frozen ice, and then we find ourselves pinched and bound, locked into tiny cells. Our cold, sharp edges become a prison. We are in here, and everything else is out there.

Understood this way, freedom is less about getting or becoming than it is about *melting*. As we loosen our grip and step into not-knowing (or at least being-not-so-sure), we have the opportunity to free ourselves from the self-imposed prison of ignorance. As we soften and melt, we cultivate the capacity to remember and return to our original, oceanic source. From there we can respond appropriately and creatively rather than reacting habitually.

Over time, the teaching that there is no separate, solid self was expanded from *anatta* to *sunyata*, the understanding that not only am I fleeting and transitory, so is everything else. This understanding is articulated through the teachings on emptiness, which (despite early [mis-]translations into English) is not a giant, empty void. Just as *anatta* does not mean no one is home, *sunyata* does not suggest there is nothing here. These teachings are not a negation of life. They are windows and doors that open us to the mystery and aliveness inherent in each moment. We, and everything we see and smell and taste and touch, are an animate web of interconnected life.

One of the most powerful descriptions of the Buddha's awakening is described in the Pali Canon as the three "watches of the night." During the first watch he saw the truth of the law known as *karma*. The word *karma* simply means "action." What the Buddha saw was how his behavior played out over many lifetimes, how actions infused with wisdom and kindness lead to helpful outcomes, whereas actions infused with greed, anger, or confusion create pain. He recognized with vivid clarity that every thought and word and deed has an impact, like ripples in a pond. He woke up to the truth that every action of body, speech, and mind shapes who we are and affects the world.

During the second watch, he saw that the law of karma applied to everyone. Just as the tone of his personal behavior colored the flavor of his experience, so, too, did the behavior of all beings everywhere. This expansion of awareness marks a movement from cognitive insight into tenderness and compassion. The Buddha saw that human suffering is universal, causing his heart to quiver and open.

In the third watch, his concentration deepened and his consciousness revealed the shape of a single moment. As he watched the moment unfold, he recognized how suffering happens and thus how it can be prevented. This third watch represents the descent of insight—starting in the mind, dropping into the heart, and finally penetrating the body, where it took root in the Buddha's bones.

The movement of wisdom from the head to the heart and then into the sinews and flesh is an apt metaphor for how intellectual understanding deepens into embodied wisdom. This insight at the heart of the third watch of the night is the heart of the Buddha's big breakthrough—the discovery that, as Buckminster Fuller once said, "I seem to be a verb." The Buddha realized that he himself, all beings, and every moment of experience is a fluid, ever-changing river of life he called *paticca samupadda,* the dynamic web of interconnectedness.

If we take this description of the three "watches of the night" as symbolic rather than literal, it suggests that insight deepens over time. Most of us imagine awakening as a single lightning-bolt event that reveals the truth of reality and delivers us into a place of final, permanent peace. But this is more wishful thinking than actual experience. Awakening is not a single event; it is a vital, thrumming process. The shape and color of reality can be realized, but it is revealed bit by bit, shifting the focus from "waking up" to "staying woke."

It is helpful to distinguish two dimensions of awakening: the content or substance of what we awaken to, and the internal experience of what the process of awakening looks and feels like from the inside. The *content* concerns what we realize about ourselves, each other, and the world. It is coming to understand who we are (and are not) and what reality is (and is not). This is the unfolding of wisdom, the clear seeing into the true nature of sentient life.

The *experience* is what it feels like to undergo the tangible, visceral transformation of having our most basic concepts and beliefs turned upside down. Although different traditions offer various maps and trajectories of awakening, individual experiences of awakening vary from person to person and even within a single person over time. It is not a single event or a singular progression.

One aspect of the experience of awakening that consistently rings through varied descriptions is that waking up is not about getting something or becoming someone; it is an ongoing process of renunciation, surrender, letting go. For Siddhartha, the process of being stripped and opened unfolds over time. When he first leaves the palace to become a renunciate, a wandering *sadhu*, he gives up his home, his family, and his identity. Over the course of many years, he wanders, studying with various ascetic and yogic masters. Images of his emaciated, skeletal body portray the extremity of his austerities. It is said that for a period of time he subsisted on only a single sesame seed each day.

Siddhartha was a star pupil, courted by myriad spiritual masters. But the teachings and practices he encountered failed to adequately address his burning questions: What is the source of human suffering? And is it possible to be free? Eventually, he let go of the harsh ascetic practices he had been offered, recognizing that denial of the body is not a viable path. But when he abandoned self-starvation and ate a bowl of rice pudding, his companions abandoned him, and he was left to find a way on his own.

The final chapter of the Buddha's story depicts him solitary and resolute, seated beneath an ancient Bo tree, determined not to get up until he has resolved his spiritual inquiry and investigation. But the story of the Buddha's path is less about willpower and solo determination than it first appears. As he teeters on the edge of starvation and self-annihilation, the bowl of rice pudding he eats is offered by a young farm girl, Sujata, who is touched by the sight of his emaciated form seated under the tree. After he takes nourishment, when he is besieged by the armies of Mara, he literally leans on the earth to support him.

The story of the Buddha reveals the fiction of solitary, heroic awakening. It is a misconception to imagine that awakening asks us to pull ourselves up by our own bootstraps. On the contrary, while the *content* of awakening may consist of insight and revelation, the *process* of awakening is rife with obstacles and struggles beyond the capacity of our singular effort.

For me the process of letting go was fraught and difficult. I did not want to leave the monastery. I wanted to commit myself to spiritual life. But that was not what happened. What happened was that I fell in love. Which was both bitter and sweet.

Eugene arrived at Tassajara during the summer guest season with his eleven-year-old daughter, Aya, in tow. The first evening, we sat across from one another at dinner, chatting over plates of tofu, brown rice, and stir-fried cabbage. His warm hazel eyes twinkled. His face was framed by soft, chestnut curls. His full mouth was etched with deep lines from years of playing the *shakuhachi* flute—lines that I wanted to reach across the table and touch. Long after our meal was finished, I wanted to stay and keep drinking him in.

The next afternoon, I found him lying on a chaise at the pool. He saw me and smiled, waving me over to take the chaise next to him. As Aya splashed and turned somersaults in the shallow end of the pool, we dove back into conversation.

Soon we were pulled out of our talk by the sound of her voice. "Dad! Dad!" Aya shouted from the shallow end. "Look at me!" We looked up as she plunged down, placing her hands on the bottom of the pool and kicking two spindly legs out of the water and into the air.

"That's great, Aya," Eugene said, smiling, and then turned back to me.

"Dad!" she called out again. "Why are you talking to her? Stop talking to her. Come play with me!"

Eugene removed his baseball cap and slid off the chaise to join her in the pool. Looking back over his shoulder, a fleeting glance ricocheted between us as we both registered a new understanding: Aya was broadcasting something neither of us had fully acknowledged.

I felt my face flush. I slipped on my sunglasses, slid into my flip-flops, stuffed my towel into my bag, and waved goodbye as I headed back to my room. I let the door click shut behind me and leaned back against the wall with a sigh, gazing up at the corrugated tin roof of my small room, feeling the tumult fluttering in my belly.

What was happening? Whatever I was feeling, it was definitely not in my plans. I wanted to stay at Tassajara, ordain as a priest, and give myself to Zen practice. I had spent hours fantasizing about floating through the world with a sheared head and flowing black robes—pristine, protected, refined, revered. I relished the dream of myself in that role.

But this was no dream. There was no way to deny the palpable energy between Eugene and me or the potent momentum that began to gather in the days and weeks that followed, through words and kisses, daily love letters that crisscrossed in the mail, and Eugene's weekend visits to my tiny room and narrow bed.

When I met with my teacher to tell him about Eugene, he beamed at me with delight. "If you are happy, I am happy, too," he said. "But you can't engage in priest training at the same time as starting a new relationship. Intimate relationships and priesthood both demand a full commitment."

I said, "But—"

He raised a hand to stop me, and for a moment our eyes met.

"I've never seen anyone do both things well," he said. "One or the other always suffers."

He paused, and a flicker of sadness crossed his face.

"And I don't want that for you," he said softly.

It was clear that there was nothing I could say to change his mind. The conversation was closed.

In a sense, the decision facing me was a simple one: monkhood or marriage? For me, the choice was clear. As my relationship with Eugene deepened, my heart opened and filled. But the process of leaving Tassajara and reentering the world was also riddled with heartbreak. The pain of letting go was wrenching, with all the agony of a breakup or divorce.

The months following my departure from Tassajara—the place, the practice, the community—brought grief that manifested as an array of physical symptoms: bone-weary fatigue; puffy, painful joints; brain fog and persistent headaches. I got tested and retested for early-stage kidney failure, Lyme disease, Epstein-Barr. But all the tests came back normal. I was relieved but frustrated. Without a diagnosis there was no hope for a cure.

It didn't occur to me that my body was expressing the impact of my heartache until I began a month-long silent retreat at Spirit Rock Meditation Center with Eugene, who was a teacher there. At Tassajara, I had been a dogged Zen student. I sat long hours, unmoving. I walked slowly, with my gaze down. I was never tempted to step out of the schedule, to read or write. I was often the first (and sometimes the only) person sitting in the hall in the wee hours of the morning, and I was frequently one of the last people to return to my room at the end of the night.

But this time, I planned to do it differently. "I'm going to take it easy," I told my friends. "I've been feeling unwell for so long, I'm taking this month away in silence as a 'spa retreat.'"

What unfolded was nothing like being at a spa.

For the first week of retreat, I couldn't stop sleeping. I slept through the wake-up bell in the morning, I took hours-long naps after lunch each afternoon, and I fell into bed each night by nine o'clock. The second week, a flood of tears descended. I cried in the hall, in my room, over bowls of oatmeal and miso soup, and as I ambled the trails around the retreat center.

Then something completely unfamiliar happened: I couldn't sit still. I moved from jumpy and agitated to disgusted and disillusioned, and from there to existential despair. The whole process felt futile. It didn't make sense anymore.

When I reported what was happening to my teachers, they were strangely affirmative, nodding knowingly and giving me pep talks. I was ready to pack my bags and go, but they kept encouraging me to stay. "What is happening is good," they insisted, suggesting that there was something good just around the corner. I trusted them, but barely. Every day I struggled, often feeling like I was barely hanging on.

Later I learned that my experiences fit a textbook description of the Progress of Insight, a Burmese map of awakening. It didn't feel like awakening—or, more precisely, it didn't feel like what I thought awakening would feel like. It felt like I was losing my mind.

At some point, the stream of experience in my mind began to speed up. A flood of dreamlike memories, images, and random thoughts and feelings were rushing through me. I tried to note and notice, but it was all moving too fast for my thinking mind to track. From the outside it looked like I was sitting perfectly still, but inside I felt like I was being swept away in a torrential river.

Then, just like my tsunami dream, a quiet voice said, *Just let go.* I softened my belly and released the clench of my fists. And then everything stopped. When my eyes fluttered open again, a knowing registered through my belly, and I heard the same voice whisper: *I am home.*

The next day, I sat outside the interview room, wrapped in a bright blue shawl, waiting to meet with the teacher. Stillness inside, stillness outside, tears of gratitude streaming down my face. When it was my turn to go in, my heart began pounding inside my ribcage, beating like a drum. I steadied myself, entered the room, and took my seat. Then I sat mute, unable to speak.

"How are you doing?" the teacher asked.

I knew something important had happened, but I could not locate the words to describe my experience.

We sat together in silence.

"Everything was moving so fast," I began. "I couldn't keep up. I didn't know what was happening. My mind, my thoughts, my body were like molecules of water in a churning river, roiling, rushing toward the edge of a cliff."

I looked up, watching him watching me.

"Then I fell over the edge," I continued.

"And then?" he asked.

"And then, well, nothing," I answered.

"Nothing?"

"Yes, it was so strange. Not like anything I'd ever experienced before."

I paused and looked down at my feet, cozy in their gray, fuzzy socks.

"Yes," I continued, "nothing happened. It was weird. A weird kind of . . . absence. Yes, absolute absence."

He adjusted his posture in the chair and waited. I didn't have anything else to say.

"And then what?" he asked.

"I'm not sure. It's hard to explain. When I opened my eyes and came back into the meditation hall, it felt like I had fallen off the edge of the planet and died. I was there but not there. I felt . . . I don't know how to describe it, more *here*, than I have ever been, but also strangely vacant."

I fell silent again, feeling the absence fill the space between us.

I said, "I felt emptied but also somehow complete. After all those days of fear and despair, it was like there was—there *is*—nothing more to do. I was done."

"What do you mean, 'done'?"

"I remember," I told him, "a voice inside said: *I am home.* That's how it felt, like being completely at rest, completely at home."

My words trailed off. We sat together in silence. It was no big deal. Me, him, us. Here. Nothing had changed, but everything felt completely different.

He leaned forward into the space between us. "What you are describing," he said, "is the experience of *nibanna, kensho,* awakening . . . the cessation of consciousness."

I raised my arms, shielding my face with my hands. "No, please don't say that!"

"Yes," he insisted, "I want you to hear this. It's important for you to take it in."

Over the next days I soaked in a profound sense of spaciousness and equanimity. Everything I saw and heard and tasted and touched felt alive, luminous, dazzling. I was brought to tears by light streaming through the branches of a tree, the soft touch of the breeze on my face, the scent of an orange, the tiny movements of a caterpillar inching across the earth. It was as if a veil had been lifted and everything was at once intimate, familiar, and utterly fresh.

"Look!" the world called out, again and again. "This! Here! Here!"

I looked. I saw. I marveled at how much magnificence I had overlooked. It felt like some kind of cosmic joke. I had been so busy trying to find my way that I had missed the truth and beauty of what had been here all along: the light, the trees, the breeze, the bugs, all as parts of me—many limbs of one giant body moving in me, as me.

A few days later, I met with the teacher again. When I shared my experience, he listened and gently guided me back toward the emptiness.

"Keep paying attention to the absence," he insisted.

"But the absence, the emptiness is full!" I exclaimed. "It is teeming, blooming, bursting, totally alive. You keep pointing to 'absent and empty'; but what I feel is 'fullness and beauty!'"

He nodded, taking in my words.

I said, "I understand that there really is nothing solid, nothing separate, nothing to grasp or grab or get. But all that emptiness is ripe with abundance. I feel in love with the whole world. Everything, everything is so beautiful and tender. Every day, every moment, there is so much *something* pouring out of nothing!"

I leaned into the space between us, gesturing with my hands. Words fell short. I wanted to show him, to conjure and evoke the paradoxical feeling of stillness and vibrancy coursing in and around me.

He leaned back in his seat.

"What you are describing sounds powerful and touching. But," he said emphatically, "it is not on the map."

His words landed like a blow to my body.

Not on the *map?*

I replied, "Then it's not a very good map, is it?"

Different spiritual maps emphasize different dimensions of awakening. But, as the Zen saying goes, maps are only "fingers pointing to the moon," words that help aim and orient us toward freedom and peace. The map, as they say, is not the territory. And if we grip too tightly—to fingers, words, concepts—we risk getting tangled in dogma and doctrine.

For thousands of years, seekers in myriad countries and cultures have been inspired by the premise and promise of freedom offered by the Buddhist path. But explanations of the Buddha's experience and of his efforts to capture, delineate, and map the shape of freedom were also imprinted by masculine cultural norms that favor wisdom, transcendence, and emptiness over compassion, connection, and the fullness of form.

There is a repeated phrase in the Pali Canon (the text that ostensibly records the original words of the Buddha) that describes awakening like this:

> *A spotless, immaculate vision of the dharma arose in him:*
> *all that is subject to arising is subject to passing away.*

When I first read this, I was stunned: *Everything arises and passes away.* Could it really be that simple and straightforward?

As our wisdom eye opens, we see into the truth of the ephemerality of life. As the Diamond Sutra declares:

> *This is how you should contemplate the fleeting world:*
> *like a drop of dew, a star at dawn, a bubble floating in a stream;*
> *like a flash of lightning in a summer cloud,*
> *or a flickering lamp, an illusion, a phantom, a dream.*

But as the sensitive, tender heart opens and we allow ourselves to be touched by each moment of life arising—as dewdrops, stars, bubbles, clouds, flickering light—in all of their mystery and magnificence, the truth of impermanence is infused with compassion and love.

Full awakening means seeing the truth of both emptiness and fullness, arising and passing. If we are humble and attentive, willing to soften and peel back the hard edges of our ideas and beliefs, the fleeting splendor and poignancy of reality reveals itself, transforming our relationship to being alive.

My favorite understanding of awakening describes this transformation as a radical shift in perspective that allows us to see the familiar world with new eyes. The poet Rumi expresses that shift in this way: "We are not a drop in the ocean. We are the ocean in a drop." When our orientation shifts, we come to see and understand ourselves, each other, and the world in entirely new ways.

One of the most radical shifts we can make is from understanding waking up as an *event* to seeing awakened life as the *expression* of beneficial qualities—generosity, patience, virtue, honesty, wisdom, lovingkindness, enthusiasm, equanimity—cultivated in our relationships with others. Here, awakening is measured not by the depth of our insight but based on our behavior: how we act and interact with each other and the world.

For me, leaving the monastery and entering into an intimate relationship became the ground in which my nascent insights could take root and bloom. The practice of formal, intensive meditation opened me to the nature of awakened reality and revealed the pearl inside me, the gem at the center of my being that had been obscured by pain, doubt, and self-hatred. But it was the grit of the world and the ache and tenderness I felt in my relationships with others that polished the pearl and made it shine. Although I gained some understanding within the pristine setting of monastic life, it was that grit that helped transform idealism and naive hopefulness into true maturity. It took diving into the fray—falling down and getting up again, again and again—to discover the wisdom that can flower from persistence and humility.

PART II

"Winning People's Hearts"

5

THE PATH IS A CIRCLE

The spiritual path does not end with awakening. Awakening is the beginning, the place from which we return to the world, reentering the familiar and the familial, moving from the extraordinary to the ordinary, from the mystical to the mundane. Walking the spiritual path is less of a straight line and more of a circle. There is no fixed end point. Round and round we go in a process of ongoing unfoldment and ripening, of stripping away, unearthing, revealing and being revealed. As we circle, insights deepen, the heart expands, and the veils of separation thin. Little by little we learn to respond with wisdom and kindness—toward ourselves, others, and the world.

After I met Eugene and before I sat the retreat at Spirit Rock, I participated in a ceremony to mark my departure from Tassajara. It was a stifling hot day at the end of the summer season. The earth was cracked and dry, and the creek was barely a trickle. The entire community gathered in the cool of the meditation hall, each monk standing in front of their seat in full robes, sweating.

I circumambulated the hall, bent over at the waist in a gesture of respect, with my knees trembling and my face wet with tears. I felt ready to leave the sheltered world of the monastery, but I was reluctant to return to the world of speed, supermarkets, and reflective surfaces.

As I completed the circumambulation, I straightened myself and stepped forward into the center of the hall, to stand shoulder to shoulder with the monk in charge of the meditation hall. He lifted an ornate silk cloth that covered a large, oblong wooden block, draped the cloth across his arm, and muttered a prayer under his breath. Then he picked up a smaller wooden block, drew a circle in the air with it, and struck the large block three times. The sharp crack of wood on wood pierced the balmy air.

"This monk," he intoned, gesturing toward me with his other hand, "having offered her effort and labor to this temple, now returns to the marketplace with gift-bestowing hands." Then he struck the block again three times. A bell sounded, and the dark-robed bodies around the edges of the hall placed their palms together in front of their hearts and bowed.

Gift-bestowing hands: hands prepared to open and offer, to share the goodness and benefit of monastic life with the world beyond the gates. My palms were damp and my fingers were clenched. *No!* I wanted to shout. *I made a mistake. I don't want to go.* Instead, I bowed to my fellow monks and followed the teacher out of the hall into the sticky evening air.

Returning to the world is at least as difficult as departing from it, if not more so. But after five years of living at the Zen center, as much as I did not want to leave, I knew I needed to test my mettle in the marketplace, to see for myself if what I had learned at Tassajara would carry me—even on wobbly legs.

I took solace in stories of the Buddha's life and his early encounters with the world after seven weeks under the Bodhi tree. One powerful story from the *Majjhima Nikaya* relates the newly awakened Buddha's encounter with a wandering ascetic named Upaka. Impressed by the Buddha's radiance, Upaka greets him and says: "You look so serene and bright! Your eyes are so clear. Your skin is so flawless. Who are you? And who is your teacher?"

"I have no teacher," the Buddha says. "I have no community. In all the world with all its gods, no one exists to rival me. I alone have reached full enlightenment. There has never been anyone like me before."

"Really?" Upaka replies. "Are you saying you are a fully awakened Buddha?"

"Yes. I am a Buddha, a fully awakened one."

The story describes Upaka shaking his head in disbelief, then turning and creeping away down a side path. After Upaka leaves, the Buddha meets a trio of past companions who had deserted him just before his awakening because he had decided to take solid food. Upon seeing him, they, too, prepare to turn away and ignore him. But, like Upaka, they are struck by his shining countenance, so instead they turn to greet and question him.

This time he tries a different tack. Instead of proclaiming his spiritual accomplishments, he introduces his old friends to a simple quartet of teachings: "There is suffering—*dukkha*—in human life," he explains. "And there is a cause of suffering: *tanha*, clinging or grasping. What I have come to realize is that freedom is possible. You, too, can be free from suffering if you engage in the path I have discovered."

Upon hearing these teachings, his companions become his first disciples.

A few months after I returned from Tassajara, I was invited to lead a small group of students in studying the dharma. The group was an offshoot of a program for spiritual activists. It included a quirky set of characters: Carmen, a young woman with a buzz cut who began her spiritual practice serving as a volunteer with Mother Teresa in India; Mary, the mother of two small girls, who started a meditation practice while going through chemotherapy; Stuart, a balding man with a round head and dimples, who lived in an ashram and was now a local community organizer; Joe, a rail-thin twenty-two-year-old who ran late-night dance raves in the city and declared himself a staunch antiauthoritarian; Joe's friend Arthur, who had a pink mohawk and wore kilts with combat boots; Pete and Dave, a couple, who wanted to bring the benefits of engaged meditation practice to their efforts to raise two adopted kids and who had offered their living room as a meeting space for our group; and Rosie, whose shock of white hair set off her piercing blue eyes and who rarely spoke.

At our first meeting, I wore robes and sat in formal Zen posture, my eyes cast down, with my hands resting just below my navel in an oval, my thumb tips touching. I bowed to the group and rang a bell to begin meditation. After thirty minutes they began to wiggle and squirm. I sat silent, unmoving. After forty minutes, Joe began drumming his fingers on the carpet, then popped off his cushion, stood up, and left the room. Mary began digging through her bag for a pen and notebook. Carmen's face flushed. Rosie continued to sit like a stone.

After forty-five minutes, I rang the bell.

"Let's do introductions," I said.

No one spoke.

I looked up to see Joe slumped in the doorway with his arms crossed, frowning at me.

Mary was writing notes furiously in her book. Pete and Dave were looking at one another with alarm. Rosie didn't budge.

"This is bullshit!" Joe exclaimed. "I'm an anarchist. I don't want to be led. Why can't we just meet and talk as equals? Isn't that what the dharma is all about?"

"I agree," Stuart chimed in. "This group feels stiff and formal. It's not what I signed up for."

"Me, too," Arthur agreed, cracking his knuckles and adjusting his kilt.

The three of them looked at each other, nodding in solidarity.

"Maybe we could hear from someone else?" I ventured.

"Maybe we should take a break for tea," Dave said. "There are drinks and snacks in the kitchen."

"I'm out of here," Joe announced. "If anyone wants to join me for a normal conversation, I'll be at the coffee shop down the block."

Dave, Pete, Carmen, and Mary scurried into the kitchen for tea, while Joe, Arthur, Stuart, and Rosie packed their bags and exited, banging the door shut behind them.

Rosie, too? I thought, feeling a landslide of disappointment in my chest. I hunched forward, shuffling through my handwritten notes. I stared down at my hands, listening to the hushed voices in the kitchen, the ticking of the clock on the wall, and the whoosh of tires on wet asphalt outside.

Then I stuffed my notes into my bag, pulled a handful of Kleenex from the box, wiped my eyes, and rang the bell. Dave, Pete, Mary, and Carmen shuffled back in with tea, taking their seats. The empty seats made gaps in the circle. The space filled with unspoken angst.

"I'm sorry," I said, "but I don't think I can do this. Please continue without me." Then I stood, bowed, and left.

A few days later I went to meet with my Zen teacher, Tenshin Reb Anderson. The teacher-student relationship is an essential component of Zen practice that defies easy categorization. A Zen teacher is neither a guru nor a friend, but someone able to see and see through a student's doubt and reflect back their essential goodness. The intimate interplay of the teacher-student relationship is formal but not stiff, tender but not saccharine, supportive but also challenging.

Sometimes the teacher's job is to receive the student's pain with kindness. Other times it is to cut through their confusion with sharp, penetrating wisdom. The job of the student is simple but not easy: to reveal their inner turmoil, to receive the teacher's feedback, and to allow their wordless beauty to be seen and witnessed.

I sat in the long hallway of the San Francisco Zen Center waiting for the bell to ring. My breath was sharp and cool. From behind the door of the meeting room came the sound: *ding, ding*. I reached over to ring the bell in front of me: *dong, dong*. Then I gathered myself and stood outside the door, scared to enter.

I took a breath, turned the handle, and stepped inside, making a standing bow after I crossed the threshhold. I looked around the room, taking in shelves of old texts lining the walls, two peach-colored tulips drooping from a vase, and the rich scent of incense rising from the bowl on the altar. My teacher sat unmoving as I made three full prostrations, placing my forehead onto the floor, before standing and then sitting again, crossing my legs beneath me.

We sat facing each other, nearly knee to knee. I scanned his face, searching, and then looked away. I laced my fingers and placed them in my lap. A single drop of sweat rolled down the side of my ribcage.

"My mind is spinning like a top," I said.

"Then let it spin like a top," he replied.

A small puff of air escaped from my mouth, making a soft grunt. I thought, *He has no idea what it's like to live in a world where everything moves too fast, there is too much to do, and never enough time to get it done.*

His eyes remained cast down.

I watched the tiny stitches of his robe rise and fall as he breathed in and out, and then I joined in, breathing with him.

After several long minutes I spilled the sad story about my failure with the dharma group.

"I just don't think I can do this," I said. "I'm too young. I don't have enough training. I'm not skilled enough." Relief flooded through me as I confessed. He listened but didn't respond.

"I can't do it," I said. "It's too much for me to take on."

He raised his gaze and looked out the window. I looked too. Outside, the sun was shining; tender green leaves were emerging from the branches of a giant oak tree.

He turned back to face me. "Don't say you can't," he told me. "Say 'I want to, but I don't know how.'"

"But I don't want to!" I exclaimed.

"Just try saying it."

I glared at him, took a stiff inhale, and tried again: "I want to . . ." I mumbled, and then stopped.

I tried again: "I want to," I said, looking him in the eyes, "but I don't know how."

He smiled.

"You can continue with the group or you can stop," he said, "but don't stop wanting to learn and grow."

I repeated his words silently inside and smiled.

We locked eyes for a moment, and it seemed like the whole room—the books, the tulips, the incense, even the long branches of the oak tree outside—smiled too.

Ah, I thought, *this is why I keep coming back.*

Several years after I left the monastery, Reb invited me to join him for two weeks of a three-month intensive period of practice at Tassajara. I juggled my schedule of work and stepparenting to make it happen, imagining myself seated in the hall in my robes, silent and still, sipping cool breaths of fresh Tassajara air.

But as it turned out, returning as a visitor was painful. My fantasy of ease, poise, and composure quickly dissolved, slipping through rough hands, leaving me chafed and raw.

I was not the only part-time visitor. My teacher had also invited a small group of other senior students, my friends and colleagues. But they were part of a group that met monthly—without me. I had asked to join and had been repeatedly turned down. "The group has been meeting for a decade," they told me. "It's closed now. We know and like you, but we are not taking in any new members." I understood, but I still felt excluded.

During the rare hours when casual conversation was permitted at Tassajara, I found myself fielding the same question over and over again: "Oh, are you here with the dharma group?" a resident would cheerfully ask. "No," I'd say, grimacing, "I am *not* part of the dharma group." After several days, what had begun as the dull ache of exclusion swelled to become a throbbing pain. I carried the sting of rejection like an injury, furrowing my brow and curling my shoulders forward in an effort to protect my heart.

One evening as I sat on my cushion in the meditation hall, I could hear peals of the group's laughter rolling out of the abbot's cabin and pouring through the cracks of the shoji screen windows. It was twilight, crisp and cool. Fall was turning to winter. As the last rays of light diminished, quiet descended through the valley.

But my heart pounded in my chest like a fist. I drew in long strings of breath with each inhalation, trying to calm the riot unfolding inside. I did not want to be mad. I did not want to be sad. I wanted to be peaceful and contented. I berated myself for my inner churn and lack of gratitude. I was here, after all. Why couldn't I just enjoy and appreciate my good fortune?

An image of the scene in the cozy cabin arose in my mind: my teacher, his attendant, and all of my friends, seated in a circle of cushions in the warm glow of kerosene light, the pungent scent of incense and lemon verbena tea filling the space. Laughter erupted amid the cheerful banter floating across the creek. I batted it away as if it were a mosquito, but the shrill buzz continued. *Inhale. Exhale.* I clenched my jaw and bore down with my teeth, willing it away.

It was no use. A wave of fury washed through me. I remembered myself in junior high, slumped against the back wall of the gym, watching awkward boys and girls slow dancing. I felt the fullness of my yearning—the desire to fit in, to be liked. I felt the rip in the fabric of belonging, seared open by my long-buried pain. I imagined myself chopping my friends up into tiny pieces, my hands stained red, quaking. I imagined flinging my dismembered friends into the creek and watching as they floated away.

The sound of someone coughing snapped me out of the grisly scene in my head. I opened my eyes. I heard and felt the bodies breathing around me, but I felt utterly alone. My hands floated up and pressed together in prayer position in front of my chest. I twisted on my cushion, turning away from the wall, and slid off my seat, slipping out the back door of the hall and closing the latch behind me. What I was doing was completely taboo. Years of training had ingrained a clear prohibition into my bones: stay in your seat; do not leave the zendo during meditation.

I held my breath as I crept down the wooden walkway that encircled the meditation hall until I reached the top of the stairs that led down to the creek. I pressed my feet into my clogs and descended the stairs. I felt unhooked, unhinged, drifting into space. I looked back up at the hall. Shadows flickered across the window screens. I pulled my wool cap down over my forehead and walked toward the creek. I wanted to get far enough away so that no one could hear the roar erupting inside me.

I found a spot under a tree by the creek and sat on the cold ground, listening to the easy flow of water over stone. I closed my eyes and let the hum of the river carry me. I cried and cried until everything washed away. My throat was raw, the muscles in my belly ached. Then I stood, brushed myself off and walked, emptied, back to my cabin. I crawled into bed in the dark and pulled the covers up over the length of my fully dressed body.

I started awake the next morning to the sound of the bell. For a moment I couldn't remember where I was. I reached down and touched the lengths of woolen fabric covering me: oh, Tassajara. But why am I wearing my robes in bed? In a flash, the memory from the night before flooded through me. I rubbed my eyes, rose, and shuffled to the sink to splash cold water on my face. I glanced up expecting a mirror, but there was none. I wrapped myself in a wool scarf and cap and headed toward the hall.

Just as I began settling into my seat, I felt a tap on my right shoulder. A familiar voice whispered, "*Dokusan.*" It was Daijaku, Reb's attendant. *Dokusan* is a formal meeting with the abbot. I had asked Daijaku to put my name on the list over a week ago. Now I wished I could ask to postpone it. I felt jumbled and disoriented; I would have preferred a morning of silent sitting to make sense of last night's events. But there was no easy way to delay or reschedule the meeting.

Inside the abbot's cabin it was cozy and warm, just as I had imagined. Logs crackled inside the wood-burning stove. I made my bows and took my seat. A long silence stretched between us. Then my voice began pouring out my sad story. I didn't leave anything out: the sting of rejection that felt like shards of glass, my red rage, the horror movie in my mind, flesh and blood on my hands. Finally, I related my escape from the meditation hall to weep by the creek.

He listened like a mountain, solid and still. When I was done telling the story, I waited. I was prepared to take the consequences, whatever they might be. In a decade of practice, I had never left the hall during meditation. I knew that doing so was prohibited, and angry outbursts were anathema. I was sure my fit of fury and violent imagination were clear signs of my flawed character. Certainly they revealed the depths of my spiritual immaturity.

Reb turned and poured a cup of tea from a pot resting beneath a puffy brown tea cozy.

"Would you like some tea?" he offered, extending a hand across the chasm between us.

"Yes," I whispered.

He poured a second cup for himself, and we sat, sipping together in silence. Whiffs of peppermint rose in puffs of warmth above each cup.

He placed his tea cup in front of him and tilted his body forward.

"How about if you and I create a new group?" he asked me.

I looked up, startled. I saw the play of laughter lighting up his eyes.

"And our new group will be so much better than their group," he continued, chuckling.

"Yeah!" I exclaimed.

And then we both burst into laughter.

Until that moment, I had thought I understood what it meant to be a good Zen student. But I only understood what it meant to follow the rules. It was not until I broke them that I discovered the truth lying in plain sight: nothing is outside of practice. Yes, all my hard work and good behavior counted, but it was sincerity and the courage to be myself that really mattered.

Little has been written about the struggles the Buddha must have grappled with over his forty-five years as a teacher: learning to share what he knew in ways that were accessible and true, meeting the inevitable conflicts that arise living in community, working with the strain of being a leader. But we do know that he continued to learn and grow. After his awakening, the Buddha did not emerge without flaws; he continued to mature and develop as a teacher, and as a human being.

Zen monastic practice has been described as being like rocks in a tumbler. Each rock starts with rough edges. After weeks, months, or years of being tossed and turned together with other rocks, the edges begin to smooth, and bit by bit, each rock is transformed into a beautiful, polished stone. This metaphor holds equally true for living in the world, where there are more rocks, more rough edges, more tumbling, and the potential for even more polishing. For me, the failures and fiascos I experienced after I left the monastery began to soften and polish me, smoothing the hard edges of my righteousness and arrogance, revealing suppleness and sincerity.

Humility, honesty, and generosity are natural expressions of awakened life. If we can see the world as a great rock tumbler, it becomes possible to meet the churn of daily life as opportunity. This isn't easy. Sometimes we need to pause, take a time out, meditate, call a friend, or ask for help. But as we stumble and tumble along, our rough edges become softer, and we, too, continue to mature and ripen.

Maturation and transformation do not happen automatically with age. Ripening is an alchemical process. It begins as we learn to be present with our own difficulties, and it deepens as we extend beyond the familiar into wider, more diverse, more complex circles of life. As we are stretched, our boundaries thin and blur, and we come to know for ourselves: no one of us can wake up and be free while others continue to suffer. It is just not possible.

The Buddha is reputed to have said, "If you knew what I know about generosity, you would give away part of every meal." This instruction is enacted in the formal Zen meal ceremony by giving away three grains of rice from every bowl served to be offered to the spirits and the trees.

Giving is an action. Traditional Buddhist teaching offers various categories of what can be given: things, teachings, presence, and fearlessness. We can give money, old clothes, flowers. We can share our embodied understanding of the teachings. We can give our care and attention with a smile or a phone call, or by offering our full attention as we listen. And we can engage in acts of courage and mettle: using our voices to offer honest feedback or to speak out against injustice. Any act of creativity and creation—of poetry, music, or art—is also an act of giving.

And *what* we give—rice, dollars, deep listening, fearless speech—is less important than the attitude with which it is given. In Pali, the sacred language of Buddhist texts, this is the distinction between *caga*, the impulse to give, and *dana*, the activity of giving. *Caga* is generosity, the spontaneous flickering of the heart that precedes an act of giving. Before we open and extend our hand, there is an inner impulse. As we notice these flickers, we come to trust generosity as one of our basic instincts, learning for ourselves that we are not only wired for survival; we are also wired to care and connect.

Buddhist psychology describes generosity as the "proximate cause," or most potent precursor, of happiness. This is the opposite of what we expect. Most of us think that happiness comes from *getting*, as in, "If I get what I want and get away from what I don't want, I will be happy." We imagine that if we try harder or have better luck or [fill in the blank], then happiness will be ours. But this strategy does not lead to fulfillment. It leads to repeated cycles of hope and disappointment, fueled by relentless effort and ending in exhaustion.

Brother David Steindl-Rast, a pioneer in Buddhist-Christian interfaith dialogue, puts it this way: "If you think being happy will make you grateful, think again. It is gratefulness that makes you happy." Gratitude is an attitude—a way of seeing the world with eyes of appreciation and wonder. When we allow gratefulness to fill us, it becomes natural for it to spill over and spread. In this way, gratitude begets generosity, and generosity begets giving. But, importantly, generosity cannot be forced. The heart is a tender, sensitive organ. It knows the difference between compulsory or saccharine generosity and the real thing.

At the end of each intensive period of Zen practice at Tassajara, there was a closing ceremony. Each person in the community was asked to stand, step forward, and ask a question of the head teacher. One by one we stood, bowed, and gave voice to our questions and concerns. The teacher sat in an ornate, carved wooden chair in elegant silk robes. He held a staff in one hand and a fan in the other. As we stood and spoke, he met us with words and gestures that conveyed gentleness matched with piercing intensity.

One questioner, Robert, was a sincere young man from Montana with a round head, thick eyebrows, and a rich baritone voice. He stood, bowed, and then spoke: "In the weeks I've been practicing here, I've felt my heart open more and more. Now it's time to go home, and I feel afraid. I don't want my heart to close down again." He paused as we took in his honest, resonant words.

The teacher looked directly at Robert and lifted his arm above his head, spreading the fingers of his extended hand wide open.

"Is this a heart?" he asked.

Robert shook his head *No*.

"Is this a heart?" he asked, snapping his fist shut.

"No."

"Right," he said. Then he opened and closed his fingers again and again to simulate a beating heart. "*This* is a heart."

The heart opens. The heart closes. This is the systole and diastole of human life. We may imagine that we want our hearts to stay open, but full-hearted generosity—with others and with ourselves—is all-inclusive. It is not a command. It is an invitation to meet ourselves, each other, and each moment exactly as we are.

True generosity is the willingness to *be with* ourselves, each other, and all of our experience without tinkering with it. It means that when we are sad or bored or disappointed, we allow ourselves be sad or bored or disappointed. *Being with* takes steadiness of heart. It is about learning to meet what arises with receptivity, nonreactivity, and appreciation, even—or *especially*—when we don't like it. This does not mean being passive. As we learn to say "Yes" to what is, we open ourselves to the possibility of responding with a clear "No."

"No" to intolerance, "no" to injustice, "no" to anything that tears the tender fabric that binds us.

6

ORDINARY BODHISATTVAS

The first time I saw someone wearing a blue bib at the Zen center, I thought, *What is that?* It took several months before I had enough nerve to voice my question out loud.

"It's a *rakasu*," the bald woman wiping down the dining-room table explained. I didn't know what that was, but I knew I wanted one.

A *rakasu* is a miniature version of a priest's robe (which is called an *okesa*). It is made by a student who cuts a single swath of fabric into many pieces and sews it together, stitch by tiny stitch, into a pattern resembling a rice field. Once the student completes the robe, he or she gives it to a teacher who inscribes the back with a new name for the student. The teacher then offers the robe back to the student during a formal Bodhisattva vow-taking ceremony called *jukai.*

It took several years for me to gather the courage to ask to sew one.

"I would like to receive the precepts," I said to my teacher.

"That's wonderful," he said, "but you need to *ask.*"

Confused, I tried again: "Uh, I'd like to receive the precepts . . . *from you.*"

He paused, adjusted his robes, and placed his hands in his lap. Then he looked me in the eye and said, "Pam, asking is a *question.*"

Oh.

When I tried to ask, the words caught in my throat. It felt like I was chewing gravel. My cheeks flushed, and two hot tears slid out of the corners of my eyes and spilled down my face.

"Would you . . . ?" I began. Then nothing.

"Will you . . . ?" I tried again.

I squeezed my eyes shut and took a sharp breath.

"Willyougivemetheprecepts?" I blurted.

When I opened my eyes, he was seated across from me, beaming. His face was lit as if someone had flipped on a switch inside.

"Yes!" he said.

We sat together for a few moments, soaking in mutual delight.

Then he said, "How was it different to *ask?*"

"Well, when I ask, *you* have all the control!" I exclaimed. Then I covered my face with my hands and began to weep.

"Even though you knew I would say 'yes,'" he said quietly. "Still, it's scary to ask."

"Yes," I whispered, as I wiped my eyes.

For decades I had lived with the certainty that I would not be heard, helped, or understood. Curled up inside a cocoon of false autonomy, I carefully cultivated an attitude of "I'll do it myself." I had used competency as protection, shielding myself from years of undigested disappointment and hurt. To ask for something exposed my vulnerability; it felt like a threat. But articulating that request for the precepts, actually *asking,* opened a chink in my armor and allowed love to flow in, filling the holes where fear once lived.

When I first came to practice at the Zen center, I was particularly struck by the archetype of the bodhisattva. *Bodhi* means "wise, awake, enlightened, or enlightening." *Sattva* means "sentient being." So a bodhisattva is a wise, feeling being, someone awake enough to understand the truth of our deep connectedness: that no one of us can wake up and be free while others suffer. This is the same truth that Martin Luther King Jr. described as the "single garment of destiny" that binds us together. It is the flip side of the experience of separateness Einstein called "an optical delusion of consciousness." And it is the essence of what Vietnamese Zen master Thich Nhat Hanh has described as our fundamental "inter-being."

In the Zen tradition, both lay and priest ordination involve receiving bodhisattva vows. Living by vow means living intentionally instead of habitually. Receiving bodhisattva vows means that instead of pursuing individual, personal enlightenment, an aspiring bodhisattva makes a promise to remain living in the world, working for the benefit of all beings everywhere. Instead of transcending the grit and pain of the world, bodhisattvas willingly roll up their sleeves and dive into the fray.

A *rakasu* is sewn through a series of tiny stitches. With each stitch, you pierce the fabric with the needle and thread, take a half-stitch backward, and then pull it ahead. It is like taking steps, forward and backward and forward again. As you stitch, you recite a mantra under your breath: *namu kie butsu*, "I throw myself into the house of Buddha." Stitches become steps, and the words of the mantra become a song. Through stitching and stepping and singing, the separate pieces become the Buddha's robe.

My *jukai* ceremony took place at the end of a five-day silent retreat. Because I had been in silence, I didn't know that I had laryngitis. When it was time to receive the bodhisattva vows, my voice had vanished.

"Even after attaining Buddhahood," the teacher intoned, "do you promise to keep these vows?"

"Yes I do!" I croaked with gusto.

A *jukai* ceremony also includes receiving lineage papers and a new name. The lineage paper, or *kechimiyaku,* is a single, long, origami-folded document that lists the names of your dharma ancestors—the many beings who have passed the light of the teaching from teacher to student for 2,600 years. The *kechimiyaku* is called a bloodline, referring to the thin red line connecting each name in a weaving, snake-like pattern. At the end of the line is you, with your new name added to the living stream of the dharma.

The new name I received was: Mon Itsu An Ka. *Mon* means listening. The character is an image of an ear at the gate *Itsu* is a single stroke that means both each and oneness: listening to each, listening to one. The first half of the name is instructive: *Listen to the simultaneous eachness and oneness of every moment.*

The second half of the name is descriptive. The character *An* is an image of a woman standing under a roof, at home, rooted, at peace. *Ka* is an onomatopoeia: a declaration of dynamism, alchemy, transformation. When we can listen to eachness and oneness, difference and sameness, at the same time—without falling over onto one side or the other—the impact is transformational.

When I left the monastery, I carried my vows with me into the busyness of business and earning a living. After stumbling through a series of part-time jobs, I found my way into a professional coach training company called New Ventures West. I began working at New Ventures as a trade: free tuition in exchange for two days a week in the office answering phones, sending out applications, and filing. I was a terrible office worker, hopeless at keeping track of details. I reversed numbers, lost messages, and misfiled critical documents. Fortunately, my boss noticed I was also exceptionally good at talking with people who called in to inquire about the coaching programs.

Possessing few practical skills, I leaned hard on the capacities I had cultivated in the monastery: being present, listening well, and asking good questions. I brought a keen curiosity, receptivity, and the ability to speak to the unique needs and concerns of each caller. I was steady and reliable, eager to learn, always ready to roll up my sleeves and help out. By the end of my first year, I was promoted to co-leading two-day coaching workshops. After several years, I became a lead teacher for the company's flagship year-long coaching program.

For me, coaching was bodhisattva work. It was a way to use what I had learned in the monastery to help alleviate suffering.

When I left New Ventures West, I used the punch line of my favorite Zen story to name my new business: Appropriate Response. In the story, a student comes to visit his dying teacher. "Tell me," the student asks, as he sits by his beloved teacher's bedside, "what is the teaching of your entire lifetime?" *What a question,* I always think to myself! The poor guy is dying. Give him a break. But of course, the question expresses the student's devotion. Before his teacher goes, he wants to understand: What is the essence of his hard-earned wisdom? What lives in the heart of his heart?

I often imagine the many possible responses the teacher might offer: vast emptiness, or pristine virtue, or oceans of kindness. But when he is asked "What is the teaching of your entire lifetime?" he replies: "An appropriate response."

His lifetime's teaching is not about esoteric wisdom or ethical behavior or being nice. It is the capacity to meet each moment freshly, and to respond with flexibility, creativity, and skill. This was the perfect succinct description of what I wanted to help awaken in others.

Most of us live in a tangle of our habits. We imagine we are in charge, calling the shots. But as we begin to pay attention, we see that we are caught in a perpetual cycle of grasping after what is pleasant and pushing away what is unpleasant. Bodhisattva vows offer an alternate option: the opportunity to live intentionally, to disengage from the perpetual push-pull of our reactivity, drop under the reflexive churn and splash at the surface, and sink into our depths. From here, we can begin to engage in the world from a place of deliberate, purposeful action.

Vows are not the same as goals. Goals are about doing. They are about imagining a future we want and then checking things off our to-do list as we move toward that future. But vows are about being; they are aspirational and intentional. Vows invite us to reach past what we think is doable or even possible. We don't take vows so we can check them off our list. We take them because they help us expand beyond the constraints of the familiar and the familial—because we yearn to discover what lies on the other side of the border of the egoic self.

Goals direct our actions. They help us get stuff done. Vows direct our attention: they shape who we are and how we engage in each moment.

The four traditional bodhisattva vows in Zen are impossible and endless. Aspiring bodhisattvas declare, "Beings are numberless, I vow to free them all. Delusions are inexhaustible, I vow to end them all. Dharma gates are boundless, I vow to enter them all. Buddha's way is unsurpassable, I vow to become it."

These vows ask us to commit to a life of imperfection and to be willing to fall down and pick ourselves up, over and over again. When I first encountered these vows, I thought, *These are stupid.* At that time I was mired in the perspective of accomplishment, reaching the top, getting to the goal, winning. But even as these vows made no sense to my striving mind, they touched something in my heart. Even though they made no sense, I longed to be a bodhisattva.

The Mahayana Buddhist canon depicts a colorful pantheon of bodhisattvas: Manjusri, the bearer of wisdom who rides a lion and uses his sword to cut through delusion; Avalokitesvara, the embodiment of compassion, who hears and responds to the cries of the world; Samantabhadra, the embodiment of enlightened engagement, who rides a six-tusked white elephant into the heart of the mess; Jizo, the "earth womb" who is the protector of travelers and children and helps guide beings into the underworld and afterlife; and a whole cast of others who represent facets of our shared human experience and potential.

History reveals examples of remarkable people—Fannie Lou Hamer, Abraham Joshua Heschel, the Dalai Lama, Bryan Stevenson, Ta-Nehisi Coates, to name just a few—who embody the bodhisattva archetype. In each case, their lives are fueled by the aspiration to alleviate suffering brought about by ignorance, oppression, and injustice. Although we may feel that our own activity fails to live up to these exalted standards, the bodhisattva ideal does not require profound deeds or fame. As aspiring bodhisattvas, the value of our actions lies less in their impact than in our willingness to engage with the sincere intention to support, encourage, and be of benefit.

In the Jewish tradition there is a corollary to the bodhisattva, the *lamed vavnik* or "thirty-six righteous ones." The term refers to the legend that in every generation there are thirty-six righteous people whose beneficence and meritorious action keep the world from tipping into destruction (*lamed vav* means "thirty-six" in Hebrew). The most unusual thing about the *lamed vavniks* is that they are unknown—invisible to others and hidden to themselves.

For many years I've introduced clients and students to a blended model of bodhisattva archetype and *lamed vavnik*. This is what a friend calls an "ordinary bodhisattva," a wise, sensitive person who quietly lives out their life in the world, engaging in acts of kindness and generosity. Like *lamed vavniks*, ordinary bodhisattvas don't make headlines or get a lot of press. They are obscure and unnoticed. An ordinary bodhisattva could be your taxi driver or dentist or best friend. Or it could be you.

Ordinary bodhisattvas are regular people who refuse to turn away from the truth of suffering. They stare it down with benevolence and the unrelenting aspiration to help. This is not naive or saccharine; it is not about thinking good thoughts or being agreeable. Ordinary bodhisattvas stand deeply rooted in paradox. They are able to articulate seemingly impossible dreams but are also willing to take on the real work of getting stuff done.

Learning to straddle paradox is wisdom. The eccentric Soto Zen poet-monk Ryokan put it this way in the eighteenth century:

Buddha is your mind and the way goes nowhere.
Don't wish for anything but this.
If you point your cart north when you want to go south,
How will you arrive?

Ryokan's poem captures both sides of the human condition. On one side, everything we need is already here. But on the flip side, we also need to "point our cart," to clarify what's most important to us, and keep checking in to see whether we have strayed off track. Otherwise all that already-hereness does us little good. A story about Zen teacher Suzuki Roshi captures the same idea. "You are perfect just as you are," he used to tell his quirky Western students. "And you could use a little bit of improvement." Or as the Sufi saying goes: "Trust in Allah, and tie your camel to a post."

These instructions echo the teachings of the second-century sage Nagarjuna, another Zen ancestor I was introduced to during my years at Tassajara. Known as the "second Buddha," Nagarjuna is the founder of the Madhyamaka (Middle Way) philosophy, which emphasizes *sunyata* or emptiness.

The name Nagarjuna means "king of the sea serpents." It is said that he rescued esoteric texts on emptiness from under the sea, where the Buddha had entrusted them to magical sea creatures for safekeeping. Nagarjuna is a blurry, legendary figure, hovering between history and myth. He may have been a singular, brilliant person, or he may have been several people. There is much about him we will never know. What we do know is that a series of texts appeared under his name between 150 and 250 CE that revolutionized Buddhist teachings.

The central tenet of Nagarjuna's teaching is that all ignorance is based on the mistaken belief in *svabhava* or "own-being." Nothing whatsoever, Nagarjuna insists, has separate, solid, inherent existence. Or on the flip side, everything everywhere is utterly and inextricably connected. I came to think of it this way: the statement that nothing exists is an expression of absolute truth looking through eyes of wisdom; the statement that everything is connected is an expression of absolute truth looking through eyes of love.

While Nagarjuna is most well-known for his writings on emptiness, texts attributed to him also articulate one of my favorite teachings: the Two Truths. This teaching holds that there are two concurrent realms of reality: ultimate or absolute truth, and conventional or relative truth. In the realm of ultimate reality and absolute truth, all things are empty of own-being, and everything is absolutely, inextricably connected. But in the realm of conventional reality and relative truth, we experience things as if they are singular and separate, causing us to feel distinct, isolated, and alone.

The suffering of our felt sense of separation and aloneness is called *sankhara dukkha*. It is the subtle but pervasive feeling of being estranged or alienated. I knew this feeling intimately, and almost everyone knows the feeling of being unacknowledged, misunderstood, or "not like them." This is a quality of suffering that cuts through the heart of each of us and is the basis of collective systems of prejudice, oppression, and injustice.

When I first heard the teaching of the Two Truths, I assumed ultimate reality and absolute truth were better and more profound than common dualistic reality and truth. But I was wrong. The key to the teaching of the Two Truths is that they are *both* equally valid and true. Like two sides of a coin, each needs and completes the other. Without ultimate nondual reality, our lives become shallow and meaningless. But without the relative, dualistic experience of differences and separation, we can never experience what it means to join hands and unite.

What I came to see and appreciate most about Nagarjuna's teaching was that it asks us to embrace paradox and to find our footing in the midst of ambiguity and uncertainty.

As I struggled to find my footing in the world, I used the model of the ordinary bodhisattva and the teaching of the Two Truths as my internal compass. I did my best to turn toward suffering, embrace paradox, and use everything I encountered as grist for learning. As my capacity to live in the world deepened, I began to articulate a vision for how to walk an engaged bodhisattva path right through the heart of the world.

The path is made by walking. Step by step, ordinary bodhisattvas become a bridge that connects. Step by step, we become both strengthened and more malleable. As we go, we discover fresh forms and ways of engaging that integrate masculine and feminine, spiritual and material, the exalted and the mundane.

I describe this as a process of maturing love with wisdom. The path of the bodhisattva begins with courageous, loving listening. Instead of turning away from the cries—our own, others', and the world's—we turn toward them, take them in, and allow our hearts to quiver. By doing this, we discover our wish to help. This is a wish born of love.

But wanting to help does not mean we are capable of doing so—at least not yet. As we walk, our wish ripens into capacity. The initial flickering of the heart in response to suffering is strengthened. Over time, our nascent wish to help deepens and matures with wisdom so that we are able to meet our circumstances with skill and kindness. Inhaling and exhaling, breath by breath, we learn to engage. We fall down and we get up again. We keep our eyes, ears, hearts and hands wide open, becoming ever more skillful as we go.

My articulation of walking the ordinary bodhisattva path has three stages: inspiration, aspiration, and appropriate response. The path begins with inspiration—literally breathing in a sense of what's possible. As we breathe in inspiration from outside, taking it into our own heart, it becomes internalized as aspiration—a clear call to respond. And as we engage, our efforts to meet the suffering of the world is honed and polished. Our desire to help is matured into the capacity to do.

Initially, as we are touched by suffering, instead of falling into despair we take solace in the wise, skillful responses of people we admire who have walked the path before us. We lean into the long lineage of people who have shown the way. Breathing in their resolve, audacity, foresight, and brilliance, we transform what was "out there" into inner strength, competence, and faith.

Being inspired is not about taking in something foreign. It is an alchemical process of reigniting something alive inside of us. When we feel stirred by the courage or patience or big-heartedness of someone else, we feel stirred because it touches something already here: our own goodness and nascent capacity, waiting to be remembered. We breathe in and remember our own basic goodness.

The world is rife with bad news. The reach of the media bombards us daily with words and images we might not have heard or seen in the past. Yes, knowledge is power, and being informed is good; but our media, and our human minds, tilt toward the dramatic and the negative. Stories of kindness rarely make headlines, so it takes clear intention to incline the mind toward beauty, generosity, and compassion. Sometimes we need to dig to find it.

Inspiration fills us. Once we are filled, we can exhale and extend. This is aspiration: breathing out, offering our own hopes, dreams, and wishes to the wide world around us. Aspiration is a process of clarifying what matters, of deciding which direction we want to point our cart. We listen outwardly to the cries of the world, and then we listen inwardly to our own nascent yearnings. As we listen, we begin to clarify and articulate our intentions. What do we want to do? Who do we want to become? As Suzuki Roshi used to ask his students, "What is your heart's inmost request?"

As we receive the messages tucked away in our own hearts, we begin to align our actions with the principles and practices we want to live by.

Our aspirations are clarified, and our abilities to respond with skill and kindness grow.

———————

The ordinary bodhisattva path is not a path of striving. There is no gold ring or gold star waiting for us when we get to the end. In fact, there *is* no end. As we walk this path, our habits and preferences get flipped upside down. The four impossible overarching vows of the bodhisattva are a doorway. They provide orientation and direction. When we open the door, we find ourselves standing in the familiar world but facing a new direction.

Once we step through the door, life continues to happen: relationships and work, birth and death, accomplishments and failures, heartbreak and delight, boredom and surprise. As we enter and begin walking, we take additional vows to help keep us in alignment. These vows are called the Bodhisattva Precepts, a list of behavioral admonitions that sound a lot like the Ten Commandments: "thou shalt not" kill or steal or lie or misuse sex or drugs.

But the Bodhisattva Precepts are more than a list of rules or prohibitions. They are also riddles or koans that illuminate the fundamental conundrums we face as human beings. The precept not to kill may sound simple, but it is not. Maybe it's easy not to kill other people, but what about animals and bugs? Even if we are vegetarian or vegan, there is still killing involved in getting our food. If we pay taxes to a government that kills people in wars, refuses to help starving people, or neglects to feed the homeless, are we not complicit in killing? And what about killing ideas or parts of ourselves or others we don't like? Is that not also a form of violence?

If we engage with the precepts in this way, they thrust us into living questions rather than guiding us toward a set of answers. They force us to loosen the grip of self-righteousness. They make the heart tender. When we take up the precepts as questions instead of commandments, they help us stay awake. In this way, the precepts keep us alert to our own intentions as we navigate everyday life. Living by vow creates structures that help us live up to the inspiration we hear and see and feel in those around us. It shortens the distance between us and them. And it allows us to move from knee-jerk reactivity toward true response-ability—the ability to respond to the world with clear, heartfelt intentionality.

Once I asked one of my teachers to help me unpack the phrase "an appropriate response."

I said, "What is the Chinese character that translates into the English word 'appropriate?'"

He smiled. "It's actually three characters: meet; each; teach."

To meet is to bring two separate things together, to join hands, to pray. Meeting is how we discover our belonging. To meet each is to do this again and again. We cannot meet in general. We must meet the uniqueness of each moment as it arises and meet each moment as it passes away. When we meet each moment, the moment itself becomes the teacher. We step in fully and are willing to learn. Teaching and learning go together.

But there is more. The Chinese character for "each" also appears in my ordination name as the character *itsu* (or *ichi*). So to *meet each* is also translated as to *meet oneness. Each one* and *oneness* are flip sides of uniqueness and unity, division and cohesion, divergence and unanimity—two dimensions of an unbroken whole.

This is how ordinary bodhisattvas live. We roll up our sleeves and engage complexity and ambiguity without flinching. We wholeheartedly meet yearning and poignancy and pain without turning away. We fall down and we get up, over and over again. We join hands with all beings and walk together through the tenderness and beauty of our wide, aching world.

7

PRACTICING EVERYWHERE

I didn't plan for it. I didn't ask for it. I didn't even *want* it. But when the call came, I answered.

It was the spring of 2008. I was newly unemployed, having recently left my job training professional coaches at New Ventures West. Now I was striking out on my own, full of hope, but unsure where my next rent check would come from.

One day that spring I got a call from a former coaching student of mine named Carole, an ex-marketing executive with a keen intelligence and a quirky sense of humor who was now a successful independent coach and consultant. Carole had a sense of style and grace I envied: textured fabrics that fell perfectly on her narrow frame, bold yellow ceramic beads from Kenya, a broad silver cuff from Peru.

When she asked me how I was doing, I said, "I'm good," noticing drops of split pea soup from lunch splattered across my T-shirt. "How are you?"

"I'm gooood," she said, lifting the pitch at the end of her reply so her answer sounded more like a question. "I was wondering," she continued, "would you be interested in teaching meditation to a leadership team I'm working with at Genentech?"

I felt my face brighten and my breath lift high into my chest. "Tell me more," I said.

"Well, I have this client who is a meditator, and he wants to introduce mindfulness to the rest of his team."

I tossed away my veneer of nonchalance and said, "Wow, I'd love to do that!"

"It would mean working inside a big company," she said, "and I wasn't sure you wanted to do that."

I tried again to sound calm. "Well, let's give it a try and see what happens."

What happened was a wild ride that turned out to involve more than I could have imagined.

The leadership team's off-site meeting was three weeks away. I started by ordering every book I could find about meditation in the workplace. It was a short list. The corporate mindfulness wave had not yet hit, and meditation was still considered weird, not something for regular folks working day jobs. I gleaned what I could from the few books I found and then tracked down the authors, grilling them about their experience. I drafted pages of notes, spent hours putting together folders with resources, and made a CD recording with a series of short guided meditations. And of course I recruited Carole to take me shopping. "If I am going to do this," I told her, "you have to help me make sure I've got a killer outfit."

Carole's client, Todd, was the head of the IT department at Genentech. Todd was a visionary leader with a full-belly laugh and a photographic memory. He had been hired to shake up Genentech's IT organization, which had the lowest employee satisfaction scores in the company. Todd was passionate about human development but disenchanted with customary corporate training. He was also a devoted practitioner of mindfulness.

"When my marriage broke up," he told me, "I moved from Houston to San Francisco and came out. My born-again family disowned me, and I received death threats. I was a wreck. I went to a therapist who told me, 'You need to sit.' I thought, 'Sit?!' I had no idea what he was talking about. Then he gave me a tape from Jack Kornfield, and I started a sitting meditation practice. It was a profound experience."

Todd had one of the fastest minds I had ever encountered. It was as if I could see the gears spinning in his head. If it hadn't been for his raucous sense of humor and generous heart, he might have been annoying. Instead, he was utterly compelling.

The night before the meeting, Carole and I stayed up late in my hotel suite, poring over the agenda and drafting pages of flip charts.

"Don't ask them to close their eyes," she warned.

"Why not?"

"It's too threatening," she said. "Oh, and try not to sound too woo-woo. These are IT guys. They like logic and facts."

Check. Eyes open. Don't speak in woo-woo. Be logical.

After Carole left, I barely slept, tossing and turning in the dark, worried they would hate me—or worse, that they would be bored.

The next morning, I took a shower, swigged some coffee, and put on my new outfit: crisp black dress pants, short black suede booties, and a teal-blue silk shirt. I wore my grandma Helen's white pearls for good luck, and I added an extra squirt of mousse to my unruly curls to keep them in line.

I arrived at the conference room early to set up the flip charts, distribute folders, and take stock of the space. Our hotel was in Carmel, and the room was lined with floor-to-ceiling windows that opened to wind-twisted limbs of cypress trees, rolling sand dunes, and a wide expanse of gunmetal-gray sea. Fog hovered on the horizon. I paced the front of the room, rehearsing my opening lines as the team trickled in and took their seats. They shuffled through the folders, booted up their computers, and talked shop. I listened in but could hardly understand their tech-heavy language and acronyms, replete with "Prop and Plat," "DMI," "FTP," and "CPU." By 8:25 a.m., thirty people sat at round tables with starched white tablecloths. The men wore button-down shirts with chinos or designer jeans. There were only three women.

Todd swooped in at eight-thirty on the dot and introduced me with his usual gusto. "Meditation is something dear to my heart," he told the group.

"It's what got me to where I am today." Then he made a sweeping gesture and extended an open hand toward me: "This is Pam Weiss. She's an executive coach and meditation expert who spent five years in a Zen monastery."

I glanced at Carole sitting in the back of the room and watched as her eyebrows lifted and eyes widened. So much for my non-woo-woo, just-the-facts cover.

As I stepped in front of the room, I took a moment to look around: weary, wary faces taking me in. I glanced out the window for a moment, allowing my gaze to extend across the water to the thin line where the sky met the sea. Then I looked at the faces again. This time, I saw something different. Just beneath a thin layer of apprehension were deep wells of sincerity, strain, and weariness: the same qualities I had brought with me when I first began to practice.

Now I was ready. I saw that these were smart, successful people. They didn't need more facts. They needed to be invited in, just as I had been. They needed a space where it would be okay to lay down their effort and rest for a little while. Just like I did.

I looked at the sheaf of carefully typed notes in my hand and set them down on the table beside me.

"How many of you experience stress?" I asked.

There was a wave of nervous laughter. Bodies squirmed and shuffled in their seats.

"Let me just see a show of hands."

They glanced sidelong at each other. Then, one by one, they lifted their arms into the air until every hand in the room was raised.

"Okay," I continued, striding into the center of the room, "and what *causes* stress?"

No one answered.

"Just call out examples," I said.

"Traffic."

"Bad drivers."

"Tax bills."

"Mortgage payments."

"Endless meetings."

A low chuckle spread across the room.

"My daughter's boyfriend."

More laughter.

"Worrying about my son's grades."

"My torn rotator cuff."

"My aging parents."

As the answers deepened, I stepped back and took them in again.

"Now let me ask you another question: what *is* stress?"

At first, there was nothing. I waited.

"It's when I yell at my kid for not doing his homework," a blond guy with a round head and glasses called out from the back.

"It's not being able to sleep at night," said an older man sitting off the side with his arms folded across his belly.

"Those are *impacts* of stress," I said. "But what is stress itself? We use the word all the time . . . but what is it?"

Again, I waited.

"Okay, we have to remember to keep the two parts of the equation separate," I said. "There is a *stressor.* That's some kind of trigger—traffic, taxes, meetings, pain. And there is how we *react* to the stressor. *That's* stress. Stress isn't the stressor 'out there'; it's how we respond to it 'in here.'"

I looked around. A few heads were nodding, and a handful of people were scribbling notes.

"So tell me," I continued. "What are some things you know that help *reduce* stress?"

"Vacation!"

A round of clapping erupted.

"A glass of Chardonnay."

"Two glasses of Chardonnay!"

"A long bike ride."

"Talking to someone I trust."

"Taking a breath."

"Okay," I said, laughing, "now you are talking *my* language!"

I described the cascade of chemicals that flood into the bloodstream when we imagine we are in danger. "Once upon a time, when we needed to run from a tiger or scale a tree, a big boost of adrenaline was useful," I said. "But when someone criticizes us, or we get a less-than-stellar performance review and we are up all night obsessing about it, that rush of adrenaline is not so helpful."

"We can respond to stress in many ways," I explained, "and you listed most of the common ones: relaxation, exercise, alcohol, talking to a friend. Mindfulness practice is another. It offers a set of tools you can use to help calm down and reset your nervous system. That way you can make more skillful choices in how you respond."

I paused again. "Are you willing to give it a try?"

All heads bobbed.

I asked them to close their eyes.

"We spend so much of our time outward," I said, scanning the room to meet Carole's gaze. I briefly blinked both eyes and nodded in her direction: *I've got this.*

"Closing our eyes helps bring our attention inward," I said. "And if that makes you uncomfortable in any way, no problem. Just keep a soft, unfocused gaze down toward the floor."

I led the group through a series of guided meditations and reflective exercises, ending with ten minutes of silence. "As you sit, just listen. Notice how sounds arise and pass all on their own; how hearing happens without any effort. You don't need to *do* anything. Hearing happens naturally . . . see what it's like to open, relax, and receive the sounds, just as they are. . . ."

At the end, I put them into groups of three to share with one another. "How did it go? Was it interesting? Boring? Weird? What parts of mindfulness practice were easy for you? And what parts were confusing or difficult? What, if anything, did you learn today that surprised you?"

I watched as they slid into animated conversation. As the clock rounded toward five p.m., I invited them to call out surprises and things they had learned.

"I thought meditation was some kind of hippie thing. But what we did today seemed pretty straightforward and useful."

"I am a marathoner. I can see how what I learned today will help me recover faster between runs."

"Before today, if you had asked me whether I could be silent for ten minutes, I would have said, 'No way.' But I did it. It was definitely different! But it wasn't that hard."

Between comments, they made jokes, poking fun at one another. Now that we were done, they rolled back the openness and intimacy they had displayed with one another. A wave of tenderness washed through me. I thanked them for their participation and closed the day tired but buoyant.

Afterward, Todd was effusive with me. "I can't believe you taught meditation without ever using the word *meditation!* You made it so everyone could join in. I loved it! Could you come teach mindfulness classes for the rest of my organization?"

"I'd love to," I said.

The next day, Todd cc:'ed me on an email announcement to his eight-hundred-person IT organization. "Mindfulness transformed my life," he told them. "Next month we will be offering a series of new mindfulness classes, and I encourage you to sign up."

A few weeks later, I arrived with another set of folders in a windowless room with fluorescent lights on the tenth floor of a nondescript office building. Twenty chairs were set in a lopsided circle. It was one of the most diverse groups I had ever taught, comprising IT wizards from the United States, India, Pakistan, Afghanistan, Russia, China, Brazil, Cambodia, and Iran.

At each session in the six-week series, I introduced a different aspect of mindfulness: listening to the body; listening to the heart; listening to others. "Mindfulness is about the quality of attention you bring to each moment—to yourself, to each other, and to everything you do," I explained. "It's like listening. When we listen deeply, things come alive." I walked them through a guided meditation and invited them to practice between sessions. One week I'd invite them to pause and take three breaths before booting up their computer. Another week they'd be encouraged to track their emotions as they moved through the day.

I had low expectations for what was possible in a high-stress, fast-paced workplace, because I had learned meditation in the monastery, where I sat for many hours in stillness and silence wearing long black robes and sporting a buzz cut. But I was surprised and delighted to discover I was wrong. The people in my classes were not just looking to lower their blood pressure and reduce their stress (though that happened, too). They were also looking for ways to pause, reflect, and bring broader meaning and context to what they were doing, and how and why they were doing it.

Rahim was a slender man with long limbs and thick, dark eyebrows from northern India. According to his classmates, he was a genius at untangling computer code. He had a gentle presence and a soft, lilting voice. During the guided meditations in each class, he slipped off his ergonomic office chair and onto the floor, where he pulled himself into full lotus.

At the end of the series, he told me, "I do *puja* and practice breath meditation every morning in my shrine room at home. I never even considered that I could practice meditation at work. This class taught me that I don't need to close my eyes and offer incense to meditate. I can practice being mindful when I'm working on a project, when I'm in meetings, when I'm riding the bus. Now my shrine room is everywhere."

Six months later, Todd called me into his office to talk about next steps.

"Your classes are going great," he said, with a Texas twang. "But I think only a small number of the people who work here will sign up for something with 'mindfulness' in the title." He hopped up from his chair and started pacing. "I want to create a *culture* of mindfulness in my organization," he said, gesturing with his arms as he walked. Then he turned and fixed me with an intense gaze. "You're a meditation teacher and a human development expert," he declared. "How would *you* do that?"

"Uh, I don't know," I stammered. "I don't know if anyone has ever done that before."

In 2008, offering meditation classes in the workplace was still edgy, and creating a *culture* of mindfulness was definitely outside the box. Fortunately, "outside the box" was Todd's sweet spot.

"Great!" he exclaimed, clapping his hands together with obvious glee. "If no one has ever done it, let's make it up!"

A week later, Carole, Todd, and I met in a corner conference room around a long rectangular table surrounded by whiteboards.

"I want to transform how people development is done in corporations," Todd began.

"Well, I've been part of lots of leadership development programs . . ." Carole offered.

"Not *leadership*," Todd interrupted. "Leaders are the ones who always get training and resources. What about everyone else? I want *everyone* in my organization to have the same coaching and support that Carole has given me."

"But that's not scalable," Carole said.

"Well," Todd mused, "that's our job today: to create the best human development program possible, and to design it so it's accessible to people all the way down the chain."

I thought, *I love this guy.* Then I said, "What if we create a *group* coaching process? That way we can keep the cost down and include more people."

"I love it!" Todd exclaimed. "How would you do that?"

"I don't know."

Carole said, "We could do an initial training for managers and then have them mentor the other participants."

"In my organization, the managers are often the problem," Todd said. "I want each person to be responsible for their own development."

Carole and I looked at one another across the table and fell silent.

Todd said, "Let's step back and not dive into the particulars yet. I want to talk about the *principles* that support people in learning and growing. How can we design something that is both profound and lasting? Most leadership training programs don't work very well. People go away for a day or a week, get all hyped up, and then come back and nothing changes. I want to create something with real traction. How could we do that?"

Three hours later the whiteboards were covered with lists of principles, outcomes, time frames, and flow charts. We paused and looked around at the mess of circles, boxes, arrows, and words surrounding us. Todd grabbed a red pen and underlined a series of phrases we'd been kicking around: "growing the whole person," "applied mindfulness," "developing skills and qualities," "in community," "over time."

After three more hours, our hands were smeared with dry-erase pen, the table was scattered with half-empty boxes of kung pao chicken and moo shu pork, and the sky had turned from dusk to dark. We'd filled the whiteboards and moved to flip charts, recording our key principles and the still-chaotic initial design.

"Great work!" Todd said as he circled the room, reading the flip-chart pages stuck on the windows. "What's next?"

I was thrilled but weary. At this late hour, even Carole looked crumpled. Her sleeves were rolled up, and she had removed her pointed beige sling-back pumps. I was splayed across two conference room chairs, my body slumped in one and my still-shoed feet propped up on another.

"What if Pam and I take all the flip charts and type them up?" Carole proposed, as she massaged the arch of her foot. "Then we can meet again and present you with a fleshed-out proposal."

"Can we meet next week?" Todd asked. "I'm in the midst of budgeting now, and I want to include a line item for this. I want to launch our first pilot in Q3."

Q3 was just two months away. There was a mountain of work to be done between here and there. I looked over at Carole and nodded inquiringly: *Are you in?* She smiled back and we voiced a robust, simultaneous "Yes."

Todd's face lit up, and he slapped the table with glee.

Over the next several months, Todd recruited an initial group of thirty managers into our nascent program, which he dubbed the Personal Excellence Program, or PEP for short. Meanwhile, Carole and I plotted and planned, shaping the principles laid out in our initial late-night brainstorm into a yearlong development program. We made a great team. I think in broad strokes, massaging messy, complex ideas into simple steps. She used her sharp attention to detail and refined aesthetic to ensure that everything we created sparkled and hummed.

At our kickoff event, Todd was at his heartfelt best. "We are a company dedicated to innovation and discovery," he began. "PEP is an experiment, but instead of searching for a cure for cancer, we are searching for how to create a culture of learning and development. This is a process for you—an invitation to discover how to bring your best self to work for the benefit of the patients we serve."

The impact of our experiment took us all by surprise. As momentum grew over the course of the year, the changes in the managers were undeniable. They were less guarded, more receptive, more alive. Feedback from their direct reports showed a steep increase in approval ratings, effectiveness, and satisfaction at work. When we asked for feedback from the participants at the close of the final session, one after another they stood and reported significant benefits.

Munther, a gentle, radiant Palestinian man who headed up the IT architecture team, was the last to speak. He was revered within the organization both for his warmth and for his uncanny capacity to solve complex problems. He was also humble.

"I am a very lucky man," he told me at our first coaching session. "I arrived in America from Gaza City thirty years ago with twenty dollars in my pocket. I worked the night shift at a hotel in Chicago, where, eventually, I was admitted to the university. And now look: I have a job at a great company, and I love what I do." Then he stood and started drawing on the whiteboard, illustrating his view of how PEP worked through flow charts and diagrams. I sat back watching in amazement, marveling at the clarity and accuracy of his mind.

"I've been through dozens of trainings and leadership programs over the years," Munther told us, "but none of them were like PEP. You didn't teach us *content*. You taught us how to learn."

Although we never said it out loud during the training sessions, Munther's pithy description was precisely what I had hoped would happen. We didn't fill them up with new theories and concepts. We didn't assess or evaluate or judge. We created a rich, nurturing environment with just enough sunlight and water to reinspire their love of learning and remind them how good it feels to grow.

Because we knew that PEP was unusual and we were going out on a limb, Todd hired outside consultants who conducted an impact study to measure the bottom-line results. When I met with the consultant, he congratulated me, saying: "You are definitely doing something right. We've measured hundreds of programs over the years, and your results are off the charts. The business impact for PEP is three times above the norm." I was thrilled—until he launched into a laundry list of suggested improvements. Each of his suggestions pulled PEP back toward corporate training norms, aligning us with traditional program protocols.

I pushed back, explaining that the PEP design choices we made were intentional.

"But you *have* to do it this way!" he insisted.

"Why?"

The look on his face was somewhere between perplexed and furious. "Because that's how it's always done!"

Exactly.

When I met with Todd to share the results, I handed him their glossy folder with the results and told him about their suggestions. "They want us to tie our program to existing business goals and metrics, to tie employee participation to the existing promotion process, and to engage managers in evaluating their progress," I said. "But I disagree. I think the fact that we are *not* doing those things is exactly what makes PEP powerful."

I waited while Todd thumbed through the report and then placed it on the table between us. Then he leaned back in his chair, laced his fingers behind his head, and laughed. "They just don't get it, do they?" he said. "PEP is not about business goals and metrics." He tapped his chest with his fingers. "It's about winning people's hearts."

Over the next years, PEP grew exponentially. What began as an initial pilot cohort of thirty recruited managers grew into a program with more than one hundred self-selected IT employees from every level of the organization each year. We hired additional coaching staff, trained graduates to serve as "PEPtators," and created a post-PEP graduate series. PEP spread into other departments inside Genentech, and after Genentech was acquired by the giant Swiss pharmaceutical company Roche, PEP extended across the ocean to London and Basel.

I was taken aback and even slightly embarrassed by our success. IT employee satisfaction moved from rock bottom within Genentech to number two in the company. Genentech IT was named the number two "Best Place to Work in IT" by *ComputerWorld* magazine. PEP received the Prism award from the International Coaching Federation and the Management Innovation Challenge award from McKinsey and Harvard. There were articles about PEP in publications from *Harvard Business Review* to *O, The Oprah Magazine*, and Todd and I made the rounds as speakers at conferences.

Todd's aim with PEP was not just to create a new program. He wanted to create a new template that challenged traditional thinking. He trusted that my background and training as a coach, Buddhist teacher, and ex-monastic would bring a fresh perspective to the tenets of conventional training and development inside organizations.

Instead of starting with goals and metrics, we began by asking two questions: *What is a human being? How do human beings grow?* We agreed that growing a human being is not the same as launching a new product or delivering a project on time; that the process of real human development is messier and less linear; and that growing humans is not a once-and-done event—rather, it's an ongoing process that unfolds over time.

The PEP curriculum was rooted in Buddhist principles. Drawing on the model of the bodhisattva, we began from the assumption that people are whole, not broken. This meant that our focus was to inspire engagement and expression, rather than trying to fix, force, or manipulate. We also understood that we would need to break the mold of using facts as fodder and that giving people information was not enough to create real change. We would need to involve the *whole* person—mind, heart, and body—if we wanted what PEP offered to deepen from intellectual understanding into embodied wisdom.

Buddhism describes three deepening stages of insight. The first stage arises from *hearing*—taking in new information from the outside. This is the initial "aha" we experience when we hear fresh facts for the first time. The second stage comes from *reflecting*—contemplating and applying the generic information we've heard in terms of our personal experience. The third and deepest stage occurs after we've chewed and digested the new insight so that it is no longer an abstract idea. Here, the insight we heard and reflected upon becomes fully *integrated*. What began as intellectual knowledge is now expressed through our words, decisions, and actions.

For example, when we first hear about the teaching of *anicca*—the truth that everything changes and nothing lasts—we may recognize that it is true, but it is not yet personal to us. Until we reflect on the ways this truth plays out as the aging of our body, or the loss of roles and relationships in our life, it remains an interesting idea, but it is not yet embodied. It is only after we live with the truth of impermanence over time that it begins to inform what we do.

To support the process of deepening insight, I designed the PEP curriculum to engage all three centers of intelligence: cognitive, emotional, and somatic. I designed the program content to descend over the course of the year, moving from the head down into the heart and then into the body. One of the central practices we introduced to support this descending movement was called the "three-center check-in." This practice was my attempt to modernize traditional meditation instruction I had learned based on the Satipathana Sutta, or Four Foundations of Mindfulness. The sutta describes an unfolding process of establishing awareness of the body and breath (*kaya*); of the flavor or feeling-tone (*vedana*) of each experience; of mental states (*citta*), including thoughts, plans, memories, aspirations and yearnings, worries and doubts; and of patterns of reality (*dhammas*). I wanted to teach the fundamentals but translate them into modern vernacular so they would be accessible for people in the workplace.

Each PEP session would open with a guided check-in. After everyone arrived, I would give them a few minutes to catch up and talk shop. Then I'd ring a bell, the signal for laptops to snap shut, iPhones to be put away, and Aeron chairs to be pushed back from the conference table.

Welcome everyone. Take a few moments to adjust your posture so you are upright and at ease. Then let your eyes close gently, and take a few deep, full breaths.

The buzz in the room starts to settle and still.

Now turn your attention to notice what you are aware of in the mind. Is there thinking? Worrying? Rehashing? What kind of thoughts are present?

I let my eyes close and watch the planning spin of my own mind.

As you are ready, let your attention drop from the head, the thinking center, down into the heart center, that area at the center of the chest. As you breathe in and out of the heart, notice your mood.... What feelings or emotions are you aware of? Maybe there's anxiety or frustration, confusion or boredom, or perhaps a sense of contentment. Just let whatever's here be here, without judgment, and without needing to change your experience in any way.

As we settle in together, a sense of quiet joy descends.

And finally, allow your attention to drop again, from the heart center down into the belly or body center, imagining you could fill the whole body with your awareness.... Now, what sensations do you notice? Maybe the body feels warm or cool, heavy and tired or spacious and light.... Maybe you're aware of the aliveness of the body as tingling or pulsing or aching. Or maybe there's a sense of stillness....

I notice a dull ache in my neck and shoulders; heat and pulsing in the palms of my hands.

There are no good or bad or right or wrong sensations. Just allow whatever is here to be here, just as it is....

I open my eyes, ring the bell, and invite them to share as much or little as they want about what they noticed. Initial discomfort—nervous laughter and defensive jokes—gives way to rapt conversation. As the sessions unfold, the check-ins stop being a weird exercise I make them do and become something they look forward to and even ask for. Over time, their awkwardness turns into eagerness. People who have worked together daily but often know little about each other's dreams and heartaches grow more comfortable getting to know each other in a deeper, more human way.

Another aspect of PEP that was rooted in Buddhist teaching was a three-step progression we called *select, observe,* and *practice.* At the start of each year, we invited participants to *select* a quality they wanted to cultivate in themselves, such as courage, generosity, patience, or passion. Then we asked them to use that quality as an opportunity to *observe* themselves in real time, noticing when they were able to engage their chosen quality and when they were not. This provided a kind of mindfulness lens through which they could pay attention throughout the day and begin to gather information about which circumstances (both internal and external) supported the expression of their quality, and which circumstances got in the way. Over time, they began to see patterns that informed their ability to make new choices and *practice* new behaviors.

The principle underlying this process is rooted in Buddhist psychology, which describes and promotes the cultivation of positive states of heart and mind. Buddhist teachings include numerous lists of qualities that can be cultivated: lovingkindness, compassion, joy, and equanimity (the Four Brahma Viharas); mindfulness, curiosity, determination, happiness, calm, focus, and equanimity (the Seven Factors of Awakening); and generosity, ethics, patience, wholeheartedness, meditation, and wisdom (the Six Perfections).

Instead of giving PEP participants a predetermined quality to cultivate, we invited them into a process of reflection and gathering feedback so each person could select a quality that really mattered to them. Our aim was to ignite passion and engagement by tapping their intrinsic motivation. We were surprised to discover how difficult this was. Instead of excitement, our invitation to select a personalized quality brought suspicion and confusion. They were used to attending training programs to accumulate new data, enhance their résumés, and climb the corporate ladder. It took a while for them to believe we were up to something entirely different.

"Can I just ask my boss what she thinks I need to work on?" they would say.

"No. The idea is for you pick something that matters to *you,*" I would reply.

"But how do I know if I'm picking the *right* quality?" they would ask, full of anxiety.

"There is no 'right' quality," I would answer, watching their eyes widen and their faces cloud over with confusion.

"Here's the secret," I would explain: "It doesn't really matter *what* you pick. What matters is that you find something meaningful enough that it inspires you to engage. *What* you pick is less important than *learning to pay attention*." To me this seemed clear and simple. For them it was a radical reorientation.

My original group of thirty managers named themselves the A-Team. They were smart and ambitious, eager to do whatever was needed to hone their skill sets, improve their performance reviews, and stand out. So when Todd invited them to participate in PEP, of course they agreed. In our first meetings they were polite and well-behaved but also wary. The whole time, I felt as if they were looking over their collective shoulders, waiting to be evaluated or criticized. I watched them scramble to look good, do what I asked, and prove their mettle.

"PEP is about learning and growing," I would say. "It's about authenticity, not performativity. There are no 'right' answers here. The more you are honest and real with me and with each other, the more you will get out of this."

Initially they weren't convinced. At each session, they tested the waters, checking to make sure there were no sharks circling underneath. It took about three months before they began to trust me and open up.

At the close of my fourth meeting with the A-Team, Carlos pushed his chair back from the table and looked me in the eye. "Do you mean it? Are you really saying that this is not for Todd . . . it's for us?" The fact that Carlos was comfortable enough to express his doubt signaled a shift. I was no longer the suspect outsider trying to sell them something they weren't sure they could trust. I met his gaze and looked around the room at the others. All eyes were fixed on me, watching and waiting. I capped my dry-erase pen and placed it on the table, squaring my shoulders to turn and face the group straight on.

As I paused to search for words, a memory arose: me seated in front of my Zen teachers, asking them—*imploring* them—"Please, tell me what to do!" I remembered my hot tears and the frustration I felt when they refused to give me answers. How frightening it was that they kept lobbing my questions back at me, insisting I find my own way. How raw and vulnerable I felt.

"Yes," I said quietly. "I really mean it. I don't care what your boss thinks, or what Todd thinks. I want to help you discover what matters most *to you.*"

I wanted to offer them a taste of what I had experienced in the monastery: the possibility of being held in a safe, nurturing environment, a place where honesty and vulnerability were valued more than looking good. For me, the challenge at the heart of PEP was to translate the heart of Buddhist teachings into a potent, user-friendly process that didn't require anyone to close their eyes or shave their head. My job was to reconfigure traditional meditation and to move mindfulness off of the cushion and out of the shrine room, into the nitty-gritty of daily life.

To do that took time, tenderness, and patience. There were no shortcuts. It took a while for them to shift out of fear, judgment, and evaluation into genuine curiosity, discovery, and insight. But once their trust was ignited and their inner flame was lit, their learning process went into hyperdrive, and the word about PEP spread like wildfire. By year two, we didn't need to do any recruiting. The word was out, and each new PEP cohort was larger than the last. In fact, we stopped recruiting and asked prospective participants to apply to the program.

What I discovered in working with hundreds of people who went through PEP over the years was a deep hunger. I found that just beneath the surface of knowing, accomplishing, and getting things right is the longing to explore, wonder, and be surprised. Most of us are eager to drop beneath cognitive understanding into something closer and more intimate; to let social pleasantries morph into real conversation; to peel back the layers at the surface and allow ourselves to be real and to be revealed.

This eagerness, it turned out, was the secret sauce of the program.

The participants thought PEP was about developing new skills and capacities. I thought PEP was about introducing covert mindfulness. And

PEP did both. But what surprised us all was not the individual growth and development it fostered; it was the kinship that arose. PEP became a form and format for growing authentic relationships and building community. It helped erase the hard lines of separation and isolation people felt, and it facilitated true cooperation, connection, and compassion. As we collected participant feedback over the years, the single most consistent affirmation we heard was: "It was wonderful to find out I am not the only one who struggles. I feel so much less alone."

Every year, Todd gave the opening talk at our annual PEP kickoff event, bringing his blend of humor, sincerity, and wisdom to inspire the new participants. Each time he opened by saying to them, "PEP is an experiment. Together we are rewriting how corporate development programs are done."

In the middle of Todd's opening talk in the fourth year of the program, Davis, one of the original A-Team recruits (now serving as a PEPtator), raised his hand.

"Excuse me for interrupting," he said, "but you've been at this for a while now. PEP has grown and spread. You have heaps of hard data and tons of anecdotes and personal stories to prove how effective it is."

Davis paused to glance over at me and then fixed Todd with his gaze.

He said, "Isn't it time you stopped calling it an 'experiment'?"

One hundred pairs of eyes looked from Todd to Davis and back to Todd again.

"'Experiment,'" Todd replied, "is a state of mind."

Not everyone found our experiment appealing. After Todd left Genentech, he brought PEP along with him to several other companies. But my efforts to introduce PEP to potential new clients often failed.

One of these was Paula, an old friend of mine in a new role: the head of training and leadership development inside a huge multinational company. She was a lively, freckled woman from New England with large, round eyes and thick red hair. She called to invite me to dinner while she was in town for her annual company conference: three days in a windowless conference room, watching hours of PowerPoint presentations and eating plates of overcooked chicken and overdressed salad. Our night out together was her reprieve.

After several glasses of sake, she confessed: "Every year it's the same thing. We bring people together from all over the world to figure out how we can get better results from our training programs. It feels like beating a dead horse."

"Well," I mused, "maybe you need to ask a different question. Maybe what's needed is something other than training."

Her response was abrupt and angry: "I am responsible for a *billion*-dollar training budget," she informed me. "Training is my bread and butter. If there is no training, I am out of a job." That was the end of the conversation. Paula signaled for the check and called a cab to take her back to her hotel.

Many other conversations about this topic followed a similar trajectory. Although it was an open secret that many corporate training programs have limited "stick," when I introduced PEP as an alternate possibility, I often ran into rigidity, fear, even anger.

There's an old Sufi story about the wise fool, Mulla Nasrudin. One evening, while out for a walk, a man comes upon Nasrudin crawling on his hands and knees beneath the glow of a streetlight.

"Did you lose something?" the man asks.

"Yes, I lost my keys," the mulla replies.

So the man joins Nasrudin in his search. After half an hour of fruitless effort, he turns to Nasrudin and asks: "Are you *sure* this is where you lost them?"

"Oh, no," Nasrudin cheerfully replies. "I dropped them up the road."

"Then why are you looking *here?*" asks the man, exasperated.

"Well, it's dark where I lost them," Nasrudin explains, "and the light is much better here."

The dark can be scary, brimming with the unfamiliar. But darkness is also the place where fresh ideas are born. During the early years of PEP, I came up with a metaphor: "It's like we're all walking around looking at the sky through a straw," I would say. "Is that the sky we see? Sure it is. Is it the whole sky? Absolutely not." Living within our tiny circle of sky can feel cozy and comfortable. Inside is everything we know: our habits and opinions, our familiar point of view. But at some point, the edges of our straw-circle stop feeling comfortable and start feeling constricting.

What I learned from PEP is that we all yearn for a bigger sky. But we don't always know how to find it.

8

EVERYTHING CHANGES

This was my moment.

There were two hundred people—speakers, seekers, and the press—piled into the old hops barn at a biodynamic vineyard in Northern California for a three-day conference. I had spent months preparing for thirty minutes on stage, to share the story of PEP.

I clipped on my mic and set down my notes. I looked out across the faces of the audience seated in front of me. I glanced back at the giant screen behind me, which showed an image of a tree trunk with mottled gray bark and wide green leaves, inscribed with the words, "Listening to the Sycamores." I was here to talk about PEP, but when my friend Anna invited me to come, she warned: "This is not a sales pitch for PEP. You need to tell a personal story."

I said to the audience, "So how did a middle-class Jewish girl from Berkeley, California, end up in a Zen monastery?" And then I told the story of my diagnosis and the battle to make peace with my body. I conjured a picture of life at Tassajara: "Imagine me with a buzz cut, wearing long, draping black robes," I said, grinning. I talked about the sounds and the silence: bells and drums, blue jays and stones underfoot, the background splash and burble of the creek. I described my confusion when the sound of the creek changed overnight from a tinkle to a roar, and the old monk telling me: "It's the sycamores."

"Yes, there is a scientific explanation for what happened," I said. "But that doesn't begin to capture the sense of amazement and wonder I felt. Not then, not now—almost two decades later."

I paused.

"I think the reason the memory of those trees has stayed with me for all these years is because it reveals something we all know but are often too busy to remember: that we are part of a shimmering web of life, a web that connects the trees to the creek, and us to the trees, and all of us to each other and to the world."

When I looked out, every face was rapt.

"So I have lots of data to 'prove' that PEP is successful. I can give you stats about improved employee satisfaction and engagement, and increased ROI. But none of that is what made PEP tick," I explained. "What is at the heart of PEP is the understanding that if we quiet ourselves and take the time to listen, we have the opportunity to remember the truth of our deep interconnectedness."

I glanced back at an image of a spider's web sparking with dew, spread across the screen behind me. I looked out and watched a woman in the second row bent over her notebook, scribbling notes.

I said, "So I'd like to give you a direct taste of this, of how to listen deeply."

I waited.

The note scribbling stopped.

"Let your eyes close gently, and take a few deep, full breaths," I said. "Let your attention settle into the immediacy of the felt sense of the body."

I let my own eyes flutter shut and felt the soft air filling my chest, expanding my ribcage. Then I continued to walk the audience through a guided meditation, encouraging them to listen intimately to sounds and sensations, thoughts and emotions.

"You don't need to change or fix or *do* anything," I told them. "Just relax. Receive. Allow. See what it's like to let whatever is here be here and be *known*, just as it is."

As my own mind and body settled, I could feel the entire room settle. There was a palpable stillness. I opened my eyes and looked out at a room filled with bodies, breathing. I rang the bell, letting the pitch of the sound reverberate and fill the space.

"As you are ready, you can open your eyes...."

When I looked out again, I saw that the face of the woman who had been scribbling notes was now damp with tears.

I placed a hand over my heart.

"Thank you very much for your kind attention," I said, making a small bow.

I unclipped the mic, gathered my notes, and made my way offstage back to my seat. The room was still, but I was buzzing. I glanced down the aisle and saw my friend, Anna, gesturing for me to step outside. I stuffed my papers into my backpack and hunched forward as I shuffled out, trying to avoid blocking the view for the people in the row behind me.

I pushed open the heavy wooden door of the barn and stepped into a blast of hot air. Anna followed me out and we stood together, blinking in the sun. I felt a pull inside, seeking feedback, hoping for praise. But when I looked into her face, I saw lines of tension pinching around her eyes. She squinted at me with a strained smile.

"I am so sorry," she said, waving her cell phone in the space between us. "Eugene has been in a serious bicycle accident."

An image of Eugene, chafed with road rash and limping off the road, floated through my mind.

Oh, Eugene, I thought.

Anna said, "They airlifted him to the trauma unit in Santa Rosa about thirty minutes ago."

I stared at her, noticing the edge of a peach-colored lace bra strap peeking out from under her dress. My fingers, puffy and warm just moments before, turned icy at the tips. Her mouth was still moving, but the sounds stopped, and everything fell silent. I felt myself lift up and out of my body. I looked down upon the scene from above: two women chatting together in the hot sun.

Anna ushered me away from the barn toward the parking lot and strapped me into the passenger seat of my gray Prius. Another friend, Jennifer, slid behind the wheel and began driving us south on Highway 101. Yellow hills, fat cows, and gnarled oak trees rolled by. I checked my cell phone, fiddled with the knob of the radio, looked out the window, checked my phone again. Each time my mind flickered toward images of the hospital, it careened away again. It was as if there was a thick glass wall standing between here and there, now and the future. Every time I turned to look, I banged my head.

The phone jingled. It was Eugene's friend, Vince.

"Hey, Pam, where are you?"

"I'm driving south to the hospital," I said as a strange sound erupted from inside me—something between a giggle and sob. I swallowed hard. "I should be there in about thirty minutes."

There was a break in the conversation, and then Vince began to weep.

"I'm sorry," he said. "I just can't stop crying."

Vince was not the weeping kind. Once a champion runner, he and Eugene shared a love of sports and an irreverent, playful boyishness.

I wanted him to stop.

"It'll be okay," I tried to reassure him. But the timbre of my voice was tight, and the pitch was an octave too high. I pulled the phone away from my ear and stared at the screen. "I've got to go now," I said, and pressed the red button to disconnect.

Time moved in starts and stops. Jennifer and I stared out the windshield. It was impossible to tell how long we'd been driving—ten minutes, an hour, all day?

My mind drifted back to the call with Vince. Why was he crying? And why was I not? I didn't feel sad. I didn't feel anything. My body was dull and heavy, shot through with a high-pitched buzz. Every time my mind began to recount what was happening—*I was at the conference, Anna called me outside, Eugene was in an accident, I am driving to the hospital*—it would short-circuit, unable to imagine the future.

I knew I was riding in a car. The sun was shining in a cloudless sky. The rough edges of the seatbelt pressed across my lap and chest. That was all. The shock and impossibility of what was happening kept me strapped firmly in the present.

Jennifer pointed to the green highway sign outside. "We're almost there," she said, as she aimed the car off the highway onto the exit ramp. We pulled into the parking lot, unbuckled, and stepped outside the car. The blacktop was hot and spongy, pulling at the bottoms of my feet. Long windows and rows of lavender lined the walkway to the front door. Flags snapped in the breeze overhead.

Jennifer held the door to the ER open to usher me in. I placed my hands on my hips and stopped, unable to move forward. She placed a hand on my shoulder and guided me toward the waiting room.

I scanned the room as I stood in line. An old man in a wheelchair, wheezing. A woman with a baby sleeping in her lap. Two kids in matching blue terry cloth gym suits using crayons to draw lopsided houses and giant robots.

"Next!" the woman behind the window called out.

I stepped forward. "I'm here to see Eugene Cash," I said.

She adjusted her glasses and peered down, scanning a list of names on the paper in front of her.

"He arrived by helicopter," I explained, hearing the same awkward, high-pitched sound that had eked out of me in the car.

She pointed me toward a pair of swinging doors to the left. I pushed them open, and someone in a white coat greeted me on the other side and led me down a long, fluorescent-lit hallway. I stopped at the threshold of the ER and tipped my head inside. A man in pale green scrubs was bent over a body with scraped red limbs, embedded with gravel and dust. Tubes snaked from his arms. There was white plastic collar circling his neck.

The doctor craned his neck to look at me. "Are you the wife?"

"Yes."

He raised a hand with a plastic glove smeared with blood and waved me in. I inched into the room and stood off to the side of the bed. Eugene lay still, with his eyes open but unfocused.

"Well, he banged himself up pretty good," the doctor said. I watched as the doctor's white plastic hands pulled a curved suture needle through the torn skin of Eugene's nose. When he finished stitching, he peeled the gloves from his fingers and tossed them into a bin on the floor.

"He broke a bunch of ribs and punctured his lung," the doctor said. "And he has a serious concussion, possibly a brain injury." There was a gaping red hole in Eugene's cheek. His eyes rolled left and right. He was making sounds, but not words.

I thought, *A brain injury?*

"Do you know who this is?" the doctor asked Eugene, leaning over his face and motioning toward me. I forced an overly bright smile and leaned in. Eugene creased his forehead and squinted.

"Emerald sky?" he asked.

My nervous laugh erupted as a whimper, and I searched the doctor's face for reassurance. A shadow of distress flickered across his eyes. I watched as he opened to absorb the rawness of my pain and then shuttered closed again.

I liked him. He seemed sturdy and adept, with a soft face beneath a veneer of gruff and stubble. I wanted to trust that everything would be okay in his capable hands.

"I think he will be fine," he said, "but it's too early to know."

I gripped the cool metal bar on the side of the bed and looked down at Eugene. My eyes landed on the hole in his cheek. I winced and my mind veered away. I pictured myself seated at a long, wooden picnic table in the sunshine where, just a few hours ago, I had been dining on organic cheese and freshly picked greens from the garden. I squeezed my eyes shut.

I wanted to be anywhere else but where I was.

Buddhism emphasizes the truth of impermanence *(anicca)*. Everything changes, nothing lasts. I knew this. Hours of meditation had revealed the simple, potent truth of fleeting moments, arising, abiding briefly, and then passing away. But it is one thing to understand the truth that everything changes in the relative peace of meditation; it's another thing to experience the gut punch of my life turning on a dime. A whole tangle of unexamined assumptions, ideas, plans, identities . . . poof, gone! Just like that.

"Do you have any questions?" the doctor asked.

I snapped back into the room and looked at the doctor. Maybe he was talking to someone else, someone stronger than me, someone whose world had not just shattered.

I shook my head.

"Let's go down the hall and chat," he offered.

Eileen, a friend who had ridden in the helicopter with Eugene, stepped forward. She was a nurse who had been with him on the bike ride and was still wearing her bike gear: dusty spandex and shoes with clips.

"Hi, Pam," she said, opening her arms to give me a hug.

Before we could embrace, a nurse walked in. She approached us and handed me a plastic bag.

"It's his bike clothes," the nurse said, nodding toward the bed. "We had to cut them off of him."

I pushed the bag away. "I don't want them," I told her.

Then she extended her other hand and opened it: a gold wedding band sat in her palm.

"We remove the rings in case their fingers swell up," she explained.

I slipped the cool gold band onto my finger as the doctor gestured toward the door and we filed out into the hall. Eileen's bike shoes clicked as we made our way down the corridor to the Family Consult Room.

The doctor pulled the door open and ushered us inside. Muted chairs sat beneath the fake watercolor paintings that lined the walls. The fluorescent light buzzed overhead.

The doctor and Eileen bantered in medical-speak. I drifted up and out again, listening to them converse from a spot in the corner of the ceiling.

"Do you have any questions?" the doctor asked again, startling me out of my hazy reverie.

"Uh, do I need to book a hotel room?" I asked.

The lines in his face sank and his shoulders pitched forward. I could see traces of gray at his temples.

"Yes," he said with a sigh, "that would probably be a good idea. Meanwhile, he'll be in the ER for at least a few more hours. Why don't you go get something to eat?"

There's a famous Zen proverb: *Before enlightenment, chop wood, carry water. After enlightenment, chop wood, carry water.* The path is made by walking. I didn't have the emotional bandwidth to pause and reflect on what was happening. The best I could do was keep putting one foot in front of another: talk to the doctor, book a hotel room, go get lunch.

We found a Greek deli down the block and ordered lunch. The guy behind the counter was wearing a white polo shirt that pulled up to reveal a roll of belly fat. He jiggled slightly as he prepared our food. When he lifted Jennifer's turkey wrap from the counter, it landed with a plop on the soft black mat lining the floor.

"Oh my god!" he exclaimed, with an exaggerated eye roll. "This just takes the cake." He looked at us, exasperated. "You cannot *believe* the kind of day I've had."

Jennifer and I traded wry smiles as he remade her turkey wrap. Then we headed outside to the patio with our food.

My phone rang and rang again: Eugene's friends Albert and Frank, his brother Sydney, his nephew Ivan. "He's in Santa Rosa," I tell each one. "He's still in the ER. He has a bunch of broken ribs, a punctured lung, a concussion, possibly a brain injury. He doesn't know where he is. He doesn't know who he is. He doesn't know who I am. It's too early to tell if any of that will come back."

Between calls, I pushed hummus, olives, and chicken skewers around on my plate.

"Pam," Jennifer said, leaning forward, "you need to call Aya."

I didn't want to call Aya, now a successful stage actress living in New York. "But I don't know what to say."

"The only thing you need to tell her," she said, "is that he's not going to die."

He's not going to die.

I punched Aya's number into my cell phone.

"Hi, Aya, it's Pam," I said to the machine. "Um, I have some bad news. Your dad was in a bad bicycle accident. He's in the hospital, with a concussion and a bunch of broken bones. Maybe a brain injury." I unclenched the phone for a moment and rubbed the palms of my hands down the front of my jeans.

"And, uh, he's not going to die."

I hung up and grimaced. Jennifer looked at me. "Good," she said.

I pushed my chair back from the table, walked back inside the deli, and began pacing back and forth in front of the tall, damp glass doors of the beverage cooler filled with Diet Coke, Sprite, Snapple, and Miller Lite.

A few minutes later, the phone rang again. Aya's voice was thin and half an octave too high.

"What's happening?"

"He crashed," I told her. "He's in the ER. It's not good."

"Is he going to be okay?"

"Well, we don't really know yet."

"What do you mean?"

"I'm not sure."

"So what should I do?"

"I think you should fly out here as soon as you can."

Five weeks and three hospitals later, Eugene was home and slowly healing. For me, managing his recovery became a new, full-time job. I plowed through my days, fueled by adrenaline and green tea. I turned over the running of my company to my colleagues, who stepped in with aplomb. I traded client calls and marketing presentations for meeting with doctors. I transformed from business attire to sweatpants, sneakers, and wrinkled shirts. I felt stripped and worn.

My reptile brain was on perpetual high alert. I walked on clawed feet, shifting my beady eyes, scanning for danger, assessing each person as helper or hindrance. Despite copious amounts of red meat and red wine, my cheeks hollowed, and my skin was parched. "I feel like my cells are unplumped," I told my friends.

This was a whole other level of letting go: releasing my identity as successful business woman and coach, and trading it for weary wife and 24-7 caretaker. Becoming a caregiver was a different kind of spiritual training. Instead of rising early to the clanging of the wake-up bell, pulling on my robes, and heading to the meditation hall, every morning I woke up in the guest room of our friends' home in Berkeley, slipped on my clothes, and drove the darkened highway to the hospital. Like my time at Tassajara, I followed a simple schedule: get up, go see Eugene, engage with the medical staff, eat, fall into bed exhausted, repeat.

Each morning I arrived at the brain rehab unit in Vallejo by six a.m. I cracked open the door to Eugene's room, never sure what I would find. His bed was a cage of nylon mesh. They zipped him in at night to make sure he didn't fall out. There was no structural damage to his legs or spine, but the blood splattered across his brain had erased his ability to balance or walk. He teetered like a child, needing to relearn each step.

Some mornings I found him curled on his bed, still sleeping. But often he was sitting upright, cross-legged and naked. As I stepped into the room, he would greet me from inside the mesh.

"Sweetheart!" he would exclaim in a toddler's pitch, his eyes wide. "Where have you been? Oh, I've been waiting and waiting for you! Where were you? I'm so glad you are here."

I would drop my bags, unzip the cage, crawl inside, and curl into him.

The window seat in the room was a makeshift altar. Buddha statues, photographs, poems, flowers, and cards sat side by side with bags of cashews, dried prunes, Smooth Move tea, green drinks, and cans of coconut water. I posted photos of pre-accident Eugene—wearing hip glasses and a baseball cap—on the wall so the staff could see that he had not always been this skinny, ornery, jumbled person.

A few close family members and other loved ones—Aya and her husband, Josh; Eugene's nephew, Ivan; and a handful of Eugene's closest companions—became the hub around which a wide web of friends, colleagues, and students circled. People from around the world sent cards, poems, flowers, CDs, prayers, picnic baskets full of food, and once, six fresh, home-baked apple pies for the nursing crew.

We created an elaborate schedule of "Eugene-sitters"—people who came to be at his bedside in four-hour shifts. We set up a website to provide daily medical updates. We fundraised to support his loss of income and help pay for the care we would need after returning home.

For me, this process involved learning about the flip side of generosity. Instead of *giving*, I was forced to practice the much more difficult task of *receiving;* saying yes and yes again, to the care and compassion that flooded our way.

Eugene's wounds began to heal, and his mobility increased, but his progress was incremental and nonlinear. There would be a few days of improvement followed by a regression. He'd be able to take a few steps unassisted, and then he'd fall and have to go back to his wheelchair. For a few days he would recognize doctors and remember the names of friends who came to visit, but then they would slip away again. In the morning he would be friendly and affable, but by evening he would be wrapped in bitterness, irritated and inconsolable.

I was Eugene's lifeline. Even when others were there, he would tug at my sleeve and draw me into the giant bathroom. "I need to talk to you. Alone," he insisted, pulling the door shut behind us.

We stood together in the sharp fluorescent light. He tottered and grabbed my arm to balance. I leaned over to shut the lid of the toilet so he could sit. Then he began a familiar round of pleading: "Can we go to a different hotel?" he would ask. Or, "Can we leave now? I want to go home. I don't like it here."

"Not yet," I would promise, "but soon." I had no idea when.

The teachings of impermanence and not-knowing I had learned in the monastery sank in deeper under the glaring fluorescent lights, beige linoleum floors, and pastel walls of the hospital. Eugene's future—and mine, by proxy—did not look good. I took solace in Bodhidharma's "don't know." Navigating my days, I silently chanted a mantra: *it will not always be this way.* I leaned hard into the truth of mystery and change, and I did my best to let it inform and buoy me.

I was not always successful.

At five p.m. I would depart, leaving him in the hands of the evening sitter and night nurse. One day at five I walked from the building to the parking lot, found my car, climbed inside, and pulled out my cell phone. A few precious moments of time alone.

As I scanned through the messages, I heard footsteps approaching.

Tap, tap, tap.

A round body in pale blue scrubs was standing outside my window. "Are you leaving?" the woman asked, peering down at me. I understood that she wanted my parking space. But I wasn't ready to leave yet.

I shook my head and looked back at the phone screen.

Tap, tap, tap.

"When?" she said, gesturing toward the oversized pink wristwatch circling her plump wrist.

I shrugged.

"Soon?" she said.

"I. Don't. Know," I said through the glass, quickly averting my eyes toward the phone again.

"Cunt," she spat, and turned away.

I flung the phone onto the seat beside me, swung the door open, and lunged out of the car.

"What did you say?" I screamed at her back.

She turned to face me: a short woman with caramel skin, wearing gray Uggs. Her hair was streaked with thick blond highlights, her eyebrows plucked into thin, arched curves above her eyes, causing her face to look perpetually startled.

"What did you call me?" I yelled.

I watched her coiled energy sink down through her legs, as if she was preparing to spring. Her eyes locked onto mine. "You want to come after me, bitch?" she taunted, curling her curved, painted nails into a fist that she slammed into an open palm. She bounced slightly from foot to foot. "Come on!"

My feet were suddenly leaden, cemented into place on the warm asphalt.

"Get away from me," I growled, a low snarl snaking up from my belly.

She made a light lunge toward me, half swinging a clenched hand.

I held her in my gaze as I screamed, "Get away from me! Get the fuck away from me! Leave me alone!" My voice cracked in a shrill pitch, piercing the evening air. I wanted to tear at my hair, snarl, claw.

"Get away!" I yelled—to her, to the walls of the parking lot, to the doctors and nurses, to everyone who was ignorant and content, continuing to live a normal life.

Then I turned and retreated, letting my body fall back into the driver's seat as I slammed the door behind me. My hands shook as I gripped the steering wheel. I looked in my rearview mirror and saw her seated in a white Chevy Silverado, gunning the oversized motor, which had me trapped in place. I sat, firm and defiant, staring out the windshield. *You can sit there as long as you want,* I muttered under my breath. I refused to move.

I heard the door of the truck open and the pounding of feet approaching again. I heard a thump and turned to see frozen blue Slurpee sludge dripping down my back window.

I waited.

A door slammed. The motor revved. I heard the screech of wheels as she peeled away, leaving broad black skid marks on pavement behind me. I lifted my arms, crossed them in front of my face and slumped forward across the steering wheel. As I released my weight onto the wheel, the car horn sounded, and I let out a long, torrential wail.

After a month, the community of Eugene-sitters had thinned. There was no one who was able to take the overnight shift. So I did.

I tucked myself into the pullout chair-bed next to Eugene's cage and listened to him breathing. He was sleeping soundly. I placed a hand on the nylon mesh and folded the other hand across my eyes. Light from the hall-way streamed into the room, along with a steady hum of sound—footsteps, murmuring voices, clanking, beeping. I lay awake, wishing for the respite of slumber. At home I took pills to help me sleep, but here I needed to stay alert enough to wake up in case Eugene needed to sit up, sip water, eat a banana, go pee.

Just as I began to doze off, I startled awake again. What was that noise? A low moan, like the dull howl of an injured animal. I sat up and looked around. I listened, but the sound had stopped. In a flash, I understood: the howling was mine.

I can't do this, I thought. *I have to go home.* I was terrified to leave Eugene alone. Would he lash out at the night nurse and wind up in restraints? Pry open the zipper of the cage, fall and break a bone? What if he slipped and banged his head? I could not leave. But I could not stay. For a few long moments I was unable to move.

Then I rose, straightened the bed in the dark, packed my bags, slipped on my shoes, and tiptoed out of the room, twisting the handle of the door to prevent it from clicking behind me.

I approached the nursing station to inform the night nurse I was leaving. "No one is with him tonight," I said. "Please check in on him." The nurse glanced up, nodded, and turned back to her computer screen. I shuffled down a long pastel hallway, turned the corner, and aimed toward the eleva-tor. I pressed the down button, felt my knees wobble, and slumped against the wall. When the elevator arrived, I pressed *L* for lobby and descended.

As the doors opened, I heard a liquid rush of music. I looked up to see a slender, brown man in a navy blue sweater with fraying cuffs and a graying beard bent over the grand piano. His eyes were closed and his body swayed as his fingers swept over the keys.

My bags dropped from my shoulders and I allowed the full length of my body to slide down the wall behind him. I sat on the cool floor, legs outstretched, eyes shut, taking in the sound. I listened, enthralled.

As the notes poured through me, I imagined Eugene in bed upstairs. Then I opened my eyes and looked at the pianist. I imagined that he, too, was here visiting a mother or a brother or a son; someone he loved lying in a bed upstairs after a stroke, or a car accident, or a fall. I pictured him sitting beside them in the harsh fluorescent light, reaching over to straighten a blanket, adjust a pillow, stroke a cheek. As his nimble hands poured out sorrow across the keyboard, a quiet warmth traveled across my chest, and I let the bittersweet notes wash through me—sadness and beauty mixed with my tears.

The dual twines of *dukkha* (suffering) and *sukha* (happiness) joined together as a single thread. Yes, there was bitterness and pain. But when I could *be with* my suffering all the way to the bottom, it opened, revealing the Buddha's breakthrough teaching of *paticca samuppada:* the truth of interconnectedness, and the sweetness of communion.

After five weeks, we returned home, and I was on a ninety-minute leash. That was how long it took before Eugene panicked and began dialing my cell phone. "Pam, where are you? I need to talk with you. When are you coming home?"

The familiar territory of home lit up neural pathways that had lain dormant within him for more than a month. Every day, he recognized and remembered more and more. But we no longer had backup staff, and as Eugene's brain began firing more consistently, he also became picky. His moods were still fickle, prone to steep and dramatic swings. One moment he was gracious and chatty, and the next he was plunged into paranoia. "Who stole my socks?" he barked, sending me into a frantic search. I would find his things—socks, bank statements, an iPhone charger—stashed away in the back of a drawer or tucked under the rug in a meager effort to hide them from the revolving circus of people passing through our home.

Sleep was elusive for both of us. He dozed off in forty-minute bouts and then woke overheated, shedding his T-shirt, sweatshirt, and sweatpants, only to pile the layers back on again when his temperature descended. The comfort I found spooning into his curved backside was broken by fits of thrashing, churning, throwing off the covers and yanking them up again.

Every morning I woke up to a pile of damp, crumpled clothes on the floor next to the bed, testimony to another night of agitation and the wild swings of his physical and emotional disequilibrium.

I grew bone weary. Everyone told me I needed to take a break. But I resisted. Finally, a friend insisted that I go with her on an afternoon outing to get a massage. Lying on the table, I began trembling and sweating. What if he falls and hurts himself? I sat upright and lied to the masseuse: "My husband is in the hospital. I need to leave now." I scrambled off the table like a scared animal, fumbling in the semidark room to dress myself. I grabbed my purse and clicked the door shut behind me, silencing the flow of smooth New Age guitar and drums.

Days and nights blurred into a sleep-deprived haze until I discovered Eugene's bottle of Xanax. It did nothing to ease his angst, but one small pill allowed me to sleep through the night or to meet his tantrums and meltdowns with an amiable calm. It was like raising a child. Every few weeks he gained a decade, moving from toddler to adolescent to young adult. With each new phase, I had to adapt my care strategies. One week I cut his vegetables and fed him. The next week he wanted to do it himself.

Walking was our big adventure. At first we only made it up and down a single flight of stairs. Then we made it out the front door and onto the pavement, and then halfway up the sidewalk. Eventually we got all the way down the block and across the street into the lush green of the park.

We shuffled along together, stooped, arm in arm, stopping so Eugene could catch his breath, or pausing to sit on a bench in the park and watch the sky. He leaned into me for support and balance, and I bore his weight as a gift. The memory of not-knowing whether he would ever walk again or talk again or be able to feed himself remained right at the surface.

Look! I wanted to shout to the cars, to the trees, to the passersby. *Look! He is walking!*

Eugene's suspicion and frustration were balanced by wide-eyed innocence and childlike purity. As we ambled together through the park, he would stop, turn to me, and wonder out loud: "Am I a meditation teacher?" Or, "How many children do I have?" And: "Are my parents still alive?"

"Yes, you are a meditation teacher," I told him. "And you have only one daughter."

Then I turned to face him, holding his shoulders between my hands. I looked into his eyes. "But sweetie," I told him, "your mom and dad are no longer alive. They died a long time ago." I watched his face as he absorbed my words, and then I folded him into my arms as he wept fresh tears for the death of his parents. It was as if he was grieving their loss for the first time.

Step by step, he recovered. Or, as he would often explain: "Recovery is the wrong word. I'm back, but I'm not the same person." It was true. His transformation was dramatic and replete with surprise. Mine was less dramatic but cut just as deep. We navigated the journey together, hand in hand, but neither of us was the same when we emerged on the other side.

People often asked me how my practice affected the journey. The truth was, I was too tired to think about practice. But the momentum of my years of training helped me navigate the days, weeks, and months of bottomless fatigue, and it took the edge off my periodic bouts of fury and grief.

In the *Sallatha Sutta,* the Buddha describes the difference between people who practice and people who do not. When a nonpractitioner runs into a difficult experience, he explains, they "worry and grieve, lament and beat their breast; they weep and are distraught." It is as if they were struck by two arrows. The first arrow is the inevitability of difficult experience: physical pain, mental distress, illness, loss, death. The second arrow is our *reaction* to our experience. It's all the ways we judge ourselves and worry and doubt: *I'm a bad caregiver. What did I do to deserve this? I must be doing something wrong.*

The first arrow is hard enough. But most of us don't stop there. We ply ourselves with dozens of extra arrows.

Buddhist practice didn't protect me from the first arrow. It didn't help me keep an even keel, make prudent decisions, or always be kind. I was far from perfect. But, most of the time, I didn't pile on. I didn't add extra arrows to an already arduous situation.

During my years leading PEP I used an adapted version of Joseph Campbell's hero's journey as a framework for graduate programs I created. I simplified Campbell's twelve-step process to just five: the Call, the Departure, the Struggle, the Awakening, and the Return. Whereas Campbell's map and perspective were distinctly masculine, in an effort to establish gender neutrality I renamed it "the *Human* Journey."

After studying myths and stories from different landscapes, languages, cultures, and religions around the world, Campbell discovered a universal pattern he called the "monomyth." It begins when the hero is called to adventure. Responding to the call, they leave the familial, familiar world and set out on a journey where they encounter trials and temptations. They struggle to the edge of death but are ultimately victorious, and they return home triumphant, bearing gifts. Examples include Odysseus, Psyche, Luke Skywalker, Bilbo Baggins, Jane Eyre, the Lion King, Princess Merida, and Shrek.

Even the myth of the Buddha follows this pattern: Siddhartha leaves home, struggles, attains awakening, and returns with the hard-won wisdom of insight and understanding, which he offers as the gift of his teaching.

For PEP, the map of the Human Journey offered a powerful antidote for traditional head-centered, content-heavy corporate training. It provided a context for understanding human development as an ongoing process rather than a one-off check-the-box event. Yet even in my attempt to be inclusive, it was still based on a masculine standard, emphasizing a solitary, independent process of overcoming difficulties through acts of bravery and fearlessness.

It is easy to use Campbell's steps and stages to map my journey as Eugene's caregiver: the Call that came through Anna's cell phone; the Departure from the familiar world of busyness and business into the labyrinth of hospitals and traumatic brain injury; the Struggles I encountered with exhaustion, anger, despair; the Awakening of tenderness and mother-bear ferocity in me; and the transformation I embodied as I Returned to the everyday and shared what I had learned with others.

But my journey was not heroic. I never donned a cape, carried a sword, or leapt from tall buildings. I was not a superhero or a saint. If anything, the transformation in me was antiheroic. I was alternately angry, despairing, delighted, and drained. Mine was a journey of being pinned in a corner and stripped to the bone. It took me far beyond my well-honed strategies and left me reeling and undone. In the process, it was not archetypal masculine capacities of courage or strength or will I discovered, but the feminine qualities of receptivity, connection, and compassion. My journey was one of profound surrender.

A more appropriate model for my journey is found in the ancient Sumerian myth of Inanna, Queen of Heaven and Earth. Like mine, Inanna's journey of descent, recovery, and restoration carries a distinctly feminine flavor, revealing the truth of interdependence and the power of love.

Inanna's story begins:

> From the Great Above, she opened her ear to the Great Below.
>
> From the Great Above, the Goddess opened her ear to the Great Below.
>
> From the Great Above, Inanna, Queen of Heaven and Earth, opened her ear to the Great Below.

As Inanna listens, she hears the wailing of her sister, Ereshkigal, Queen of the Underworld, who is mad with grief over the death of her husband.

"I am going down," Inanna announces, despite the chorus of worry and angst that greets her declaration. Everyone knows that no one returns from the Underworld. But Inanna is resolute, and she sets forth on her journey of descent.

The beginning of the myth reveals a feminine twist. Inanna's journey starts with compassionate listening, the willingness to attend to the shadowy Underworld, where cast-off parts of ourselves churn and fester, unexamined. The direction of Inanna's journey is also telling. She does not set out across the wide world; rather, she descends, dropping down into the depths of what is already here.

What does it mean to descend and discover more about who we already are? What does it take to unearth previously ignored aspects of our heart-mind and weave them into wholeness?

As Inanna travels down, she passes through seven gates, where she is stripped of her royal accoutrements—silken robes, lapis lazuli beads, brass breastplate, golden scepter—until she arrives at the court of her sister, "naked and bowed low." When Ereshkigal sees Inanna, she immediately strikes Inanna dead and hangs her body on a meat hook.

The story is not over yet because Innana's journey is not a solitary effort. After three days, her faithful attendant, Ninshubar, beats the drums of Heaven, calling for help. In response, old Father Enki fashions two tiny, magical creatures—the *kurgara* and the *galatur*—from the dirt under his fingernail and sends them into the Underworld to help her.

I love the image of dirt as the source of magical powers and salvation. What is needed is so often right under our nose (or feet or fingernails). Also, the assistance of Ninshubar and Father Enki underscores the importance of attentive companions and of asking for help. Inanna's journey emphasizes that *while no one can walk our path for us, we do not walk alone.*

Meanwhile, back in the Underworld, Ereshkigal continues to wail and moan.

"Oh my heart!" she calls out.

"Oh your heart," the *kurgara* and *galatur* whisper, hovering close.

"Oh my liver!"

"Oh your liver."

This call and response of grief continues until Ereshkigal, now feeling much better, sits up and asks the two creatures, "Who are you? And what gifts can I offer you for your kind words? I would gladly give you the bounty of the harvest, the depth of the oceans, the vastness of the sky."

"Actually, we'd just like that body over there, hanging on the hook," they say. Ereshkigal gives it to them, and then they revive Inanna and escort her back to the Great Above.

The empathic mirroring between Ereshkigal and the *kurgara* and *gala-tur* offers a concise depiction of how to engage with painful states of body, heart, and mind. Be present with what is. No judgment. No advice. Hover close, listen, and respond with simple, honest words.

Instead of going outward into the world, Inanna's adventure takes her down, into her depths. Instead of returning home with riches and power, she returns with a rounder, more inclusive integration of who she is. This is how healing happens. Or it is a more accurate description of how it happened for me.

For many years I walked in a man's world—the world of a Zen monk, with shorn hair and androgynous robes; and the business world, with silk shirts, strings of pearls, and sensible shoes. My journey from successful businesswoman to caretaker traversed new and often unfriendly external territory, such as emergency rooms and doctors' offices. But the real journey was not attended by dramatic acts of bravery or heroism. Instead, like Inanna, my journey was one of descent, of being stripped away until I was open enough and sensitive enough to take in the care and compassion offered by a wide circle of friends and family, near and far, who listened to my cries and responded—bringing groceries, doing laundry, offering massage and yoga and acupuncture and rides—until my superhero cape was in tatters and I could no longer maintain the false narrative of going it alone.

When the Buddha is challenged by Mara, he claims his belonging by touching the earth. When Inanna is brought back to life, it is through the kindness of tiny creatures made of dirt. These stories reveal what I discovered: salvation is not about transcending upward, above the dusty world; it is a process of sinking down into the dirt and letting the dirt transform you.

The word *humus* comes from the Latin, meaning "earth" or "ground." Humus is the dark, loamy soil that nourishes and supports life. What I discovered in my journey of descent and resurrection was not steely willpower or courage. What I discovered was, in a word, *love.*

I do not mean love as a feeling or even as the quality of *metta*—the benevolence, warmth, and lovingkindness—taught by the Buddha as an antidote to fear. I mean love as an unstoppable force, love as the magnetic pull we feel toward people and things we care deeply about. I mean love as the stitches in the fabric of my *rakasu* and as the power of the dharma that

Kobun said held the teapot together all those years ago. This is the love cultivated by aspiring bodhisattvas, whose willingness to stick it out over the long haul is not fueled by fleeting emotion that easily succumbs to burnout, but is nurtured and sustained by deep understanding and profound faith.

The novelist and social critic James Baldwin described it this way: "Love takes off the masks that we fear we cannot live without and know we cannot live within." For me, it was through traversing personal crisis that I discovered what had been missing from my spiritual and professional life. Then, little by little, I found the mettle to step outside traditional masculine maps and forms that no longer fit.

PART III

No Part Left Out

9

MISTAKES THE BUDDHA MADE

Several years after I left Tassajara, I returned to visit, journeying back down the long, dusty road to stay for a week during the summer guest season. No longer a member of the community, I felt the sting of being an outsider. I was cleaner and more put together; my clothes were less ragged, my skin and dark curls were groomed with conditioners and lotions, and I wore sling-back sandals instead of flip-flops. But all that polish could not conceal the ache I felt inside.

Bumping along the road, I soaked up the majesty of the green mountains and was flooded with memories of living among them: the rustle of sycamores in the autumn, warming my icy fingers over wood-burning stoves in the winter, the cheerful yellow surprise of daffodils bursting out of dark soil in the spring, draping my body over smooth granite stones baked warm by the sun in the summer.

The stage wound up and then down, curving from the crest of the mountain into the narrow valley I had once called home. When the dinner bell rang I was loath to join the guests in the dining room to be waited on by cheerful, ragged Zen students who reminded me of my former self. I scarfed down an apple and a bag of almonds, and I fell into a restless sleep. All night I dreamt of wandering the dim corridors of a giant, windowless building. The hallways were punctuated by thick, gray doors. I stopped at each one and twisted the handle. But they all were locked.

In the morning I woke to the familiar sound of feet pounding the dirt pathway and the clang of the wake-up bell. *I used to do that,* I thought, as I pulled on my robe, shuffled along the path, and entered the zendo.

After meditation there was an abbreviated morning service of bowing and chanting. First we chanted the Heart Sutra, and then we recited the lineage of awakened masters or Daioshos (the Japanese term for "great teacher"). The names began with the six Buddhas before Siddhartha Gotama: "Bibashi Butsu Daiosho, Shiki Butsu Daiosho, Bishafu Butsu Daiosho, Kuruson Butsu Daiosho, Kunugonmuni Butsu Daiosho, Kasho Butsu Daiosho," and then continued through the names of the Indian, Chinese, and Japanese ancestors, until we reached "Shogaku Shunryu Daiosho," also known as Shunryu Suzuki Roshi, who founded the San Francisco Zen Center and established Tassajara as the first Soto Zen monastery on Western soil.

I called out the names, long ago committed to memory, taking them in as ballast.

And then something surprising happened. At the end of the Daioshos, a voice announced that we would now chant the names of the *women* dharma ancestors. The collective voice of the community began chanting: "Acharya Mahapajapati, Acharya Mita, Acharya Yosodhara, Acharya Tissa, Acharya Sujata...."

I opened the chant book to find a new page titled "Names of the Women Ancestors." When did this happen? I stumbled through the pronunciation of the first few "Acharyas" (the Sanskrit term for "teacher") and then stopped. I listened, letting the evocation of this long unseen, unnamed lineage wash through me. Then I burst into tears.

All those women. I didn't know how much I had missed them until their names were literally ringing in my ears.

One winter, while I was living at Tassajara, I sat in the meditation hall next to a visiting Japanese nun named Haruku. Her stillness was palpable. She would soundlessly slide onto her cushion and then sit unmoving: simple, solid, nearly breathless. From time to time I would glance sideways just to make sure she was still there.

Haruku practiced with us for a month, and at the end of her stay, a group gathered in the dining hall to share tea and cookies with her. In strained English, she labored to describe her life and practice.

Someone asked her, "How would you describe meditation?"

"It is like entering a secret garden," she replied.

"How is practice here different from practice in Japan?"

She paused and then lifted her arms so that her hands were in front of her with the palms facing down and the fingertips pointing toward each other.

"In Japan," she said, "men and women like this," and she raised her left hand up toward the ceiling, creating a wide gap. "At Tassajara, like this," she said, closing the gap as she brought her hands and fingers back into alignment.

Shunryu Suzuki came to San Francisco from Japan in 1958 at the age of fifty-three. After purchasing the 126-acre plot of land surrounding Tassajara Hot Springs, he became the monastery's first abbot. In Japan, men and women practiced separately in a system that favored men and treated nuns as second class. In a radical move, Suzuki Roshi created a different kind of monastery, where men and women lived and practiced side by side, sitting and bowing and working shoulder to shoulder. During the years I lived at Tassajara, equal numbers of men and women held spiritual and administrative responsibilities. The misogyny Haruku described in Japan was not apparent at Tassajara. There was no overt bias or discrimination. We were all in it together.

So my burst of tears at hearing the names of the Buddhist women ancestors took me by surprise. Until I heard the women's lineage chanted out loud, I hadn't noticed their absence—the thousands of years of women, overlooked and forgotten. As I let their names wash through me, their unspoken, unheeded struggles and accomplishments rose up in me as a deep ache. I felt the sting of their invisibility for the first time.

Most stories about the life of the Buddha emphasize his spiritual insights and attainments. But like Suzuki Roshi, Siddhartha Gotama was a social revolutionary. He lived in a highly stratified class system but eventually offered his teachings to all classes: kings, farmers, merchants, soldiers, servants. He described his teachings as going "against the stream"; against our deeply ingrained habits of personal and interpersonal reactivity, and against our shared cultural norms.

Known historical facts about the life of the Buddha are scant. We know he was born in 563 BCE in what is now Nepal. He was the son of Suddhodana, the leader of the Shakya clan. His mother, Maya, died soon after his birth, and he was raised by his mother's sister, Pajapati Gotami. As a young man, he was married to Yasodhara, the daughter of the leader of the neighboring Koliya clan, and they had a son, Rahula. At the age of twenty-nine, Siddhartha gave up his position as heir to the throne and left his family to spend six years as a wandering ascetic. At age thirty-five, he attained enlightenment, established a community, and taught until his death in 483 BCE at the age of eighty.

For several hundred years, the teachings of the Buddha were passed down in an oral tradition. By the time they were written down, their tone and flavor were influenced by the male monastic scribes who recorded them, infusing his words with bias and systematically writing women out of the story. What we find in the early written accounts of the Buddha's teaching is an overlay of distrust and disgust toward sexuality, desire, and women's bodies. These early teachings consistently depict women only as obstacles to the ascetic male ambition of celibacy and self-denial.

Whereas histories describe the events that unfolded at particular places and times, the myths and stories of the Buddha convey a different kind of truth, revealing universal archetypes that expose as much about the views and perceptions of the authors as they do about what actually transpired.

At the center of the mythic story of the Buddha recounted in the Pali language is the description of his departure from home. After his birth, a seer predicted that he would become either a great leader or a great spiritual teacher. His father, King Suddhodana, had a strong preference in the matter: he wanted his son to become his heir and inherit the throne. So he cloistered the young prince in the palace, showering him with every possible worldly pleasure in an effort to prevent him from taking up spiritual practice. In one story, it is said that the king, eager to prevent his son from witnessing anything unpleasant, sent gardeners to deadhead the roses in the royal garden at night so the young Prince Siddhartha would not see wilted or dying flowers.

But Siddhartha was curious. One day, the story goes, he snuck out of the palace. As he toured the countryside with his driver, they encountered four "heavenly messengers": an old, toothless man with sagging skin, bent and hobbled by age; a sick man with a distended belly, covered in open sores; the body of a corpse, flaccid and disfigured, with the life gone out of him; and finally, a holy man strolling peacefully beneath the shade of a tree.

These archetypal symbols of old age, sickness, death, and liberation deeply affected the young prince, opening him to the stark truth of human transience and suffering, and piquing his interest in spiritual life. They planted seeds of doubt in him about the value of his privileged life, ultimately leading him to abandon his role as heir to the throne in order to find answers to the burning questions inside him: *What is the cause of human suffering? Is it possible to be free?*

There is an alternate version of the story. In this version, after a night of extravagant celebration, the young prince woke up to find himself surrounded by sleeping partygoers, drooling and disheveled. Roused from his drunken slumber, he looked around the room where mere hours ago the perfumed guests had been alluring and attractive, adorned with jewels, dining on fine foods, engaged in dancing and lovemaking. Now he saw them unmasked, with their unattractiveness and raw vulnerability exposed. The sight caused him to be overcome by disenchantment and disgust.

This rendering of the story offers a grittier version of Siddhartha's disillusionment with worldly life. Whereas the first story conveys a dawning existential awareness of human fragility and mortality, the second story portrays the disappointment that arises when we discover that worldly pleasure fails to provide lasting happiness.

One of the most difficult stories in the Buddhist canon concerns the Buddha's complicated relationship to women. While it is clear that he offered his teachings freely to everyone and opened his *sangha* (community) to men from all social classes, women were conspicuously absent from the Buddha's *sangha*, at least in the beginning. According to various accounts, the Buddha repeatedly forbade women to join the community as nuns, and when he did allow them in, he saddled them with repressive rules of conduct, locking them into a permanent state of subservience.

The Buddha's Aunt Pajapati, who raised him after his mother's death, traveled more than two hundred miles on foot to ask him to allow her to join the community. Many stories describe Pajapati arriving with swollen, bloodied feet, her clothes in rags, her face streaked with sweat and tears, begging her nephew to admit her into his community.

Three times she asks, and three times the Buddha says no. He tells her, "Do not set your heart on this, Pajapati."

But her heart is set. The third time she visits, Pajapati brings a large crowd of women with her. While she goes to petition the Buddha, the crowd waits outside. The Buddha's trusted attendant, Ananda, hears them and looks out across the ragged sea of road-weary bodies and devoted, upturned faces. He asks them, "For what reason do you stand outside, with bare, soiled feet, your bodies covered with dust, tired?"

"We want to join you in homelessness and train in the path of awakening," they reply.

Moved by their devotion, Ananda goes to speak with the Buddha on their behalf. Often depicted as a lovable, soft-hearted figure, this time Ananda rises to the occasion, becoming a true ally who speaks for those whose voices are denied. Ananda asks the Buddha to admit the women. And again the Buddha says, "No. Do not set your heart on this, Ananda." But Ananda's heart is also set.

He asks the Buddha, "Is it true that women can attain full awakening?"

"Yes, it is so."

"And is it true that Pajapati suckled you at her breast, raising you as her own son?"

"Yes, it is so."

"Then how can you turn her and the other women away, refusing them entry into homelessness and training in the path?"

The Buddha finally relents. He agrees to allow women into the community, but with conditions: eight "weighty rules" they must observe for the rest of their lives. The most egregious of the eight rules states that even the most senior nun who has been ordained for one hundred years must bow down to and respect a junior monk even if he has only been ordained for a single day. It is unclear whether the Buddha initiated the eight heavy rules himself or if they were added later by male monastics who became the scribes and keepers of Buddhist history. What is clear is that the rules defined women as second-class citizens within his community.

It could be argued that the rules were written out of kindness because the Buddha feared for the women's safety and was concerned that nuns living unprotected in the wild would be vulnerable to physical and sexual assault. Or perhaps, having already violated convention by opening his community to men from all social castes, he was reticent to push his radical social engineering any further. We may never know the motivation for what happened. What we do know is that women were eventually able to join the Buddha's community. And we also know that attitudes of misogyny and gender bias continue to this day.

One summer, five years after I left Tassajara, I traveled with a group of friends to visit a Theravada monastery in California. We arrived, removed our shoes, and were seated in a canvas tent on burgundy-colored cushions facing a wooden platform that served as a makeshift stage. The morning was blue and crisp. The cloth walls of the tent rippled in the breeze. The monks, with shiny heads and saffron robes, entered single file, bowed to a statue of the Buddha, and took their seats. They chanted together in Pali. The potent, ancient sounds rose into the clear air.

The senior monk offered teachings. His words were simple but deeply resonant, flush with devotion and quirky splashes of humor. I listened, fully enthralled, inspired by his integrity, purity, and virtue. Based on my own years as a monastic, I felt myself drawn into an idealized, romantic view of monastic life.

After the talk, we toured the grounds in the back of a red pickup truck. As we bounced along a narrow road, our driver pointed out the monastery garden, a giant *stupa* (a dome-shaped shrine), the early stages of construction for a new meditation hall, and a handful of *kutis* (simple tentlike structures) dotted along the hillside where monks lived and visitors could come to stay. My friend Bill nudged me, pointing to a *kuti* where he had lived as a guest for a week.

"Oh, I would love to do that!" I exclaimed, picturing myself nestled inside, cozy and warm, deep in meditation. And then the image popped because I remembered that this was not a Soto Zen monastery, which meant that as a woman, I was not welcome to stay here overnight.

I fell into a pained silence. As we continued bumping along the road, the simplicity and beauty of the teachings from the morning replayed in my mind. But now I recalled part of the scene I had forgotten: while the monks held forth on stage, a group of women were scurrying about in an ill-lit kitchen, preparing tea and snacks for the crowd.

The weight of hundreds of years of disregard and disrespect landed like a lead ball in my belly. Had it always been this way? The men on stage, adorned and adored, while behind the scenes an anonymous, unsung group of women do the heavy lifting. In a flash, my nostalgia and longing shattered. Left behind was simmering rage.

A decade later, my husband and I hosted Ajahn Brahm, a senior monk in the Ajahn Chah Thai Buddhist lineage, at our meditation group at a Unitarian church in San Francisco. In 2009, Ajahn Brahm had become the first monk to oversee a full *bhikkhuni* (nun) ordination of four women in Perth, Australia. As a result, he was excommunicated and his monastery was delisted by the senior monks of the Ajahn Chah lineage.

When I met him in San Francisco, he was seated on stage, flanked on either side by Theravada nuns, all of whom were swathed in orange robes. This was a clear break from traditional protocol. In a remnant of the old "weighty rules," monks are traditionally required to be seated above both nuns and laypeople.

After offering a few opening remarks, Ajahn Brahm opened the floor for questions. For a few long moments no one spoke. I looked across the room and watched as members of the audience shuffled in their seats, reluctant to rise and come forward. Then I stood and stepped up to the microphone.

"You have done so much to support women in the Theravada tradition," I said. "Can you share with us why you chose to offer full *bhikkhuni* ordination for the nuns?"

Historical records show that the early Buddhist nuns' communities in India and Sri Lanka died out due to famine and war. Theravada monks and scholars have used this fact as a pretext to prevent reinstating full ordination for Theravada nuns. The rationale rests on circular logic: because the nuns' lineage died out, there are now no fully ordained nuns. And because there are no fully ordained nuns, it is not possible to renew the nuns' lineage.

"Listen," Ajahn Brahm said, "I am *the* expert on the *vinaya* [the monastic code of ethics]. I'm *the* foremost scholar on this topic. Before I was excommunicated, everyone came to me as the singular authority on Buddhist rules of conduct and etiquette."

All eyes were focused on him, listening.

He continued, "So whatever explanations the so-called scholar monks have come up with to deny women full ordination as *bhikkhunis,* it's all bullshit."

A few gasps and chuckles rolled through the hall. People shuffled their feet and coughed into their hands.

"I am using this language intentionally," he said, waving his hands for emphasis. "The Buddha encouraged his disciples to use informal language and everyday idiom to convey the teachings. He was not interested in rigid doctrine or dogma. He wanted to make his teachings accessible by using colloquial language."

I was still at the microphone, so I ventured further. "I am aware that by doing this, you were banished from your lineage," I said.

We locked eyes for a moment, and then I continued. "I just want to express my gratitude for your courage and chutzpah." I smiled. "That's a Yiddish word that means audacity and having a sturdy backbone."

He grinned back, looked me in the eye with a steady gaze, and said, "Sometimes you just have to do the right thing."

An ocean away, at Amaravati Monastery in the UK, Ajahn Brahm's dharma brother, Ajahn Sumedho, had behaved in a very different manner. Several months before Ajahn Brahm completed the full ordination of the nuns in Australia, Ajahn Sumedho imposed a set of strict regulations on the nuns living in his community. Sumedho's regulations were called the "five points," echoing the Buddha's original eight weighty rules. The first point states: "The most junior monk is senior to the most senior nun. This structural relationship is defined by the *vinaya* and cannot change over time." Another point unequivocally declares that nuns cannot now—nor will they ever—be granted permission to receive full ordination and become *bhikkhunis*.

To remain in the community and continue their training, the nuns living at Amaravati were obliged to agree to the five points. Recognizing that this move would be controversial, Ajahn Sumedo told them not to speak about it outside the community, and he threatened that if they did, he would banish them from the monastery.

Ajahn Sumedo did not want to expel the nuns from his community. He said, "We need nuns . . . provided they stay in their place." But in response to the five points, many nuns from Amaravati disrobed and departed, while others chose to remain in robes but relocated to less repressive environments.

Although the fallout from the five points was substantial, the story of the crackdown on the nuns' community received little press and is still not widely known. Significant efforts were made to censor and silence the female monastics and prevent their story from coming to light. Their male counterparts continue to collect ample financial support from Thai and Western donors, but many nuns still struggle to receive even the basic resources needed to survive. Bhante Gunaratana, a senior Sri Lankan monk living in West Virginia, was an early leader in championing the *bhikkhuni* order, but most Western Theravada male monastics were not. Of the hundreds of Theravada male monastics in Europe and the United States, very few—Ajahn Brahm, Ajahn Sujato, Bhikku Bodhi, and Venerable Analayo—have come forward to actively voice support for the nuns.

Since Ajahn Brahm completed his initial *bhikkhuni* ordination, a growing number of Theravada nuns have also received full ordination. Ayya Tathaaloka, an American-born Buddhist nun who received full *bhikkhuni* ordination during an international, multilineage ceremony in Los Angeles in 1997, has played a pivotal role in this process. She acted as a preceptor for the initial *bhikkhuni* ordination with Ajahn Brahm, has continued to oversee subsequent ordinations, and founded the North American Bhikkhuni Association.

In other Buddhist traditions, more women have taken positions of leadership and empowerment, with women abbots heading up Zen centers and female lamas leading Tibetan communities. But the same issues of gender inequity, harassment, and abuse making headlines in the secular world and within Western spiritual institutions are mirrored inside Buddhist communities and retreat centers.

Periodically, issues of sexual transgression or gross abuse of power come to light. But the less obvious partiality and preference for a distinctly masculine type of spiritual practice often goes unseen and unchallenged. The structure and forms of Buddhist practice and institutions in the West maintain a distinctly patriarchal flavor: they are hierarchical and are often led by charismatic male teachers, and they have a focus on teachings of emptiness and penetrating wisdom. Yes, women now hold positions of power and authority. But they do so within the context of a patently patriarchal spirituality that carries a negative bias against the body and the earth and that favors transcendence.

While secular mindfulness has taken hold in the popular culture, androcentric spiritual practice tilts toward lifting us upward, out of the density of the flesh and the grittiness of the marketplace. And the hierarchical systems within Buddhist centers continue to privilege clergy and to emphasize monastic and retreat practice over engaged practice in the world.

A more feminine flavor of spiritual practice tilts toward embodiment and engagement with the world. It focuses on transformation rather than transcendence and on staying grounded, with our feet firmly planted on the earth. It emphasizes the importance of cultivating humility, celebrating the wide, wild expression of humanity, and caring for our one shared home.

Although progress has been made in giving women power within existing patriarchal structures, there is still work to be done. Until women's experience and perspective are named, acknowledged, and given voice, the shape of Buddhist teachings and the understanding of what it means to wake up will remain lopsided and askew.

10

THE WOMEN SPEAK

Izumi Shikibu, one of the greatest poets of the *waka* style of poetry from Japan's Heian period, is known for her unapologetic, highly publicized life of love and passion. Shikibu became a fixture in the Japanese court after having affairs first with the emperor's son, Prince Tametaka, and then his brother, Prince Atsumichi. Her early poems are rich in descriptions of lust and love-play. Toward the end of her life she converted to Buddhism, and the tone and texture of her poems shifted from celebrating desire to extolling awakening.

One of my favorite awakening poems from Shikibu uses the traditional image of the moon as a symbol of enlightenment, but instead of portraying the process of awakening as austere and ascetic, she highlights the experience of fullness and inclusivity:

Watching the moon at midnight
Solitary, mid-sky
I knew myself completely
No part left out.

In the Soto Zen tradition in America, lay and priest ordination both include hand-sewing a robe by cutting a single piece of cloth into fragments and then stitching it back together again. Reparation is also a process of stitching, sewing the parts left out—women and the feminine—back into the fabric; repairing, mending, and healing the fragmented cloth into completion. To do this includes restoring sensuality, the body, and the earth, as well as the lived experience and perspective of those who identify as female.

Ursula LeGuin writes, "We are volcanoes. When we women offer our experience as our truth, all the maps change. There are new mountains." There is a difference between adding women's stories to a male-centric narrative and creating an entirely new narrative written from a feminine perspective. Adding women's stories into an existing account of things is patchwork, an act of adaptation and accommodation. Writing the story from the perspective and in the voice of women is radical revision. It is not just patching holes in the fabric; it is creating new cloth.

The women in the Buddha's life flit around the edges of his story like shadows. Vague images populate his personal narrative—of his mother, Maya, who died soon after giving birth; her sister Pajapati, who raised him after Maya's death; and his wife, Yasodhara, whom the young prince abandoned to follow his spiritual yearning shortly after she gave birth to their son, Rahula.

From a factual, historical point of view, the lives of the women surrounding the Buddha are uniquely theirs. They unfolded in a distinct time, place, and culture. But there is history and then there is myth. Each tells a story: his, hers, theirs, ours. History is truth distilled through recorded facts—what happened when and to whom. Myths tell a more finely textured truth, layering fact with emotion and meaning. Mythic stories use individual and collective experience to reveal universal patterns and archetypes. Myths do not recount what unfolds in linear time; rather, they offer insight into the underlying structures through which we know ourselves and understand the world.

From a mythological point of view, the stories of the women surrounding the Buddha are universal, describing the joys and struggles in all women's lives. In my efforts to unearth these stories, I had to sift and sort through historical data, and I also needed to discover the truth of their heartaches and insights in my own experience. In the pages that follow, as I use my voice to illuminate and express their perspectives, my intention is to offer a wider, more embodied spiritual path, and a deeper, more inclusive understanding of what it means to awaken.

I am grateful to the many women who have taken up this project over the years, excavating lost or neglected songs and stories from the long lineage of Buddhist women. As I immersed myself in researching the historical stories of Maya, Pajapati, and Yasodhara, their shadowy images came into focus. No longer minor characters in someone else's drama, they took their place on center stage as full-bodied, fleshy mountains of their own. In the morning, in the liminal space between sleeping and waking, they would come to me and recount their stories, painting a luminous picture of their lives. They spoke. I listened. Then I did my best to capture what they told me on the page.

To tell the history of women in the life of the Buddha is an act of reparation. To give texture and voice to these feminine archetypes begins to weave them back into the fabric of Buddhist teaching, to repair the rent in the cloth. This is how volcanoes erupt, new spiritual maps emerge, and we bear witness to the birth of new mountains.

Some accounts recall that the Buddha's mother, Maya, struggled for years to conceive. All of them agree that she died within a week of giving birth to her only son.

> I wake up. The palace is dark and still. I am reluctant to open my eyes, unwilling to release last night's dream, wanting to savor the fleeting memory that fills me with delight.
>
> In the dream I am seated in a green meadow under the shade of a wide shala tree. The sky is clear blue. The warmth of the sun streams through the fat leaves in long lines of golden light.
>
> A white elephant with six great tusks appears and approaches me. He circles once, twice, three times. With each labored step, his huge

feet send gentle reverberations through my body. I tremble with fear and longing.

He seats himself on the ground before me, tucking each of his massive legs under his girth. I begin to sing, caressing him with tender words. He raises his trunk and trumpets, releasing a potent blast up toward the sky. His call pierces the air and settles into my bones. I watch with wonder as he rises up from the dusty earth and enters my right side, just below my ribcage.

I feel his fullness filling me. My skin turns translucent. My breath abates. I am awash in pristine stillness: vast, radiant, untethered.

My eyes flutter open in the dark. I rise slowly and call my attendant to bring my robes. She drapes an emerald lamb's wool cape around my shoulders, brushes the length of my black hair, and bathes my feet with rose water.

I walk the long, cool corridor to Suddhodana's quarters and tell him my news. "My darling," I say, "I dreamt of a white elephant with six tusks. In the dream, he entered me."

I watch Suddhodana's face as he takes in my words. His eyes glisten. He smiles and embraces me.

"I will send for Asita," he says. Asita, the Brahmin holy man and seer, will come to interpret my dream. But we already know. After years of anguish from an empty womb, there is new life growing inside me.

Asita arrives, wearing white robes and carrying a gnarled walking stick. His matted gray hair and beard set off the creases in his face and dark almond eyes. He places his hands on my belly. He listens.

"She is with child," he confirms. "Your son is destined to be exceptional. He will either be a great ruler or a great spiritual teacher."

I watch Suddhodana's face strain as he hears Asita's prediction.

"This is cause for celebration," Asita declares. He holds Suddhodana in his gaze and says, "It is not yours to determine the fate of this child."

But I know where Suddhodana's heart lies. He wants our son to be his heir and the next king.

Weeks pass. My breasts and belly swell. I savor the heaviness of my body as pure pleasure. I am an ocean of gladness. Waves of contentment surge through me.

Months pass. The baby spreads inside me, kicking and tumbling in the salty sea of my womb. As birthing time approaches, we prepare to journey from the plains into the foothills of the Himalayas, where I will be cared for by my mother, the queen of the Koliyas.

I bid goodbye to my king. My sister Pajapati and my attendants pack the caravan, and we set out from Kapilavatsu along the dusty pathways toward the great Rohni River. I rest in my palanquin, shrouded from the heat of the day as we climb up, up toward the snow-covered mountains. I watch a cloak of thickening greenery spread across the landscape as I listen to the steady steps of the pole bearers carrying me home.

Red and purple rhododendron and larkspur burst from the fields as we climb. The leaves of spruce, cedar, and oak rustle in the breeze. The scent of wild herbs mingles with yak dung. I picture the peaked roof and whitewashed walls of my family home in Devadaha, and I imagine the warm embrace of my mother's sturdy arms around me.

Suddenly I am struck by searing pain. I clutch my swollen belly and cry out.

The caravan halts, and Pajapati enters the palanquin. When she sees the flood of waters staining my robes, she squeezes my hand. "Your time has come," she tells me.

The caravan stops and turns toward the pleasure gardens of Lumbini. It is here, and not in the arms of my mother, that I will bring my young prince into the world.

The gardens are lush green, verdant, blooming with life. Deer and peacocks wander the pathways, and the air is thick with birdsong from cranes and laughing thrushes. But the beauty of the garden is veiled behind a blur of tears and pain. My body seizes. I moan and cry out. Pajapati places my hands in hers and sings to me. My retinue circles me, placing cool cloths on my forehead, massaging my feet, chanting and making offerings to the gods.

Hours pass. I squat. I stand. I writhe. I wail. I grow weak with weariness, until I am wilted.

Pajapati supports me as I reach for the long limb of the ancient shala tree above me. I stretch upward with my arms as I squeeze down with my legs. I call up every last bit of energy I can conjure and let out a final groan as my son slides into Pajapati's arms. I collapse onto the ground, exhausted.

Pajapati cleans and swaddles the baby, laying him on my chest. I feel soft waves of breath pour through his tiny body; the quiet, steady beating of his heart. Together we fall into a weary, dreamless slumber.

I am aware of the sounds of scurrying feet, of hushed whispers, of worried words, of the cries of my baby boy. But I am unable to open my eyes. My belly is bound. My heart races, pounding. A thick stream of blood pools between my legs. I feel myself slipping away. I fall into darkness.

Pajapati was Maya's older sister, who was also married to the king. After her sister's death, she raised Prince Siddhartha as her own son. Later in her life, she was one of the first women to join the Buddha's spiritual community as a nun, where she became a leader of the *bhikkhunis* and was given the name Maha Pajapati.

I wake up. I hear the cries of my sister. She has fallen into a fever. I bind her belly to stop the river of blood rushing from between her thighs. She thrashes and cries out.

We lay the length of her weary, bloodied body on a bed of palm leaves and lift her legs so her feet rest above her head. I gently massage her belly with warm, melted ghee. We wipe sweat and tears from her face and squeeze drops of cool water from a cloth between her parched lips. But the life is flooding out of her. Her once-radiant eyes are now hollow and sunken, her full, red lips now tinged with blue. Her breath is labored and unsteady.

I listen as she takes her last breath. A brief, sharp inhale, and then nothing. Now I am the one who is crying out, my grief rising into the night air as bitter howling. I beat my breast, rip my dress, smear my face with ashes. I weep and wail until there is nothing left inside me.

A messenger is sent to inform Suddhodana. I tremble, imagining his fury and grief. But I must attend to the baby. Because my own son, Nanda, is only eight months old, my breasts are still full and heavy. I wipe my tears and cradle Maya's baby in my arms. My nipples respond to his cries by seeping breast milk. I suckle him, and he falls into a contented sleep.

It is bittersweet to grieve the loss of Maya while celebrating the birth of Siddhartha. The opposing emotions twist inside me. I am overcome by both the death of my beloved sister and the outpouring of love I feel for her newborn son.

Pajapati raised the two boys, Nanda and Siddhartha, as brothers, feeding them at her breasts, cooking them sticky rice and buckwheat, roasted pheasant, buffalo stew, and pungent cups of yak butter tea. She dressed them in fine, embroidered silks, pierced their ears, taught them how to wrap their turbans and paint their dark eyes with charcoal. She watched them grow up together as intimate companions.

When they are ten, I bring Nanda and Siddhartha to the annual plowing festival. All day, men and oxen labor in the fields under the hot sun. Nanda, simple and carefree, joins in, playing at being a laborer, tilling the ground with a tree branch and swatting at the animals. But Siddhartha stays back, taking a seat on a hillside overlooking the fields under the shade of a rose-apple tree.

When I come to gather him for the noon meal, I find him sitting upright and still, his face wet with tears. I call out, but he does not respond. As I approach I see that he has fallen into a state of meditative absorption. I place a hand on his shoulder and shake him gently. He opens his eyes slowly and blinks in the sun, staring at me as if from far away.

He says, "When the oxen till the earth with their plows, they slice and kill the earthworms." His eyes are soft, tender. "Then songbirds come and pluck the worms from the soil. As they eat, hawks swoop down and clench the birds in their beaks as they fly away...." His voice trails off. I reach for his hand, but he brushes me away.

"Everything is food for something else," he says. I nod. "But what happens to the worms, the birds, the hawks after they are eaten? Where do they go after they die?"

Siddhartha is intelligent, athletic, accomplished in his studies and pursuits. But his handsome face and muscular body mask the disquiet and tenderness he holds inside. Unlike Nanda, Siddhartha is introspective, wistful, uneasy.

I know his questions are his way of trying to make sense of the death of his mother. Her absence hangs about the palace like a shadowy secret; her name and memory are spoken only in whispers. But perhaps he is old enough now to know the truth.

I sit in front of him and recount the story of his birth and Maya's death, watching as the rhythm of his breath rises and crashes like waves breaking through him. He watches me closely as I speak. When I stop, he closes his eyes. It is as if I can see the doors and windows inside him slamming shut.

"You are the only mother I have known," he says. "Please do not speak to me about this again."

I honor his wish, but I feel Maya's absence as a chasm inside him—the silent anguish that fuels his disaffection and moodiness.

The king trained Siddhartha in the ways of the warrior caste and prepared him to become the next leader of the clan. He built three palaces, one for each season, and showered Siddhartha with every luxury. He brought him the best Brahmin tutors and taught him the arts of war. Siddhartha excelled at his studies and consistently won contests but took little delight in his studies or sporting events.

One afternoon when Siddhartha and Nanda are teenagers, they return home from hunting. Siddhartha cradles a great heron in his arms. Nanda follows behind him, sheepish and chagrined. Their silk shirts are torn and stained with blood.

"Nanda shot the heron," Siddhartha explains. "Its wing is broken. Now we must nurse it back to health."

I take the bird from him and place it on the floor, watching the faint beating of its heart.

"Siddhartha . . ." I begin.

"No!" he exclaims, stamping his feet in anger. "We must heal him."

Siddhartha sits up all night with the heron, chanting softly as he changes the bandages on its broken wing, dripping water into its beak from a twisted cloth. In the morning I find him curled on the floor with dried blood on his hands, his face smeared with dirt.

I shake him awake. Together we silently carry the heron into the garden, where we dig a shallow grave. He places the bird into the earth, offering prayers and weeping.

"That bird had my wings," he whispers. He is not addressing me. He speaks to the sky, the trees, conversing with an unseen force. "Like me," he says, "the heron wanted to fly away but could not."

When Siddhartha turns eighteen, the king calls for a festival at the palace to find a suitable wife for him. I busy myself in preparation: tending the garden, whitewashing the palace walls, and helping prepare food for a grand feast. On the day of the festival, I spend all morning greeting families from across the countryside who arrive on horseback, in chariots, and on foot. In the afternoon, I watch Siddhartha and Nanda compete in war games—archery, swordplay, horse races. In the evening I am seated next to Suddhodana in a lavish silk tent where we dine on fine foods and are entertained by singing minstrels, drummers, and dancers.

After the feast, Siddhartha sits on a throne, and the daughters of each family line up to greet him. The line snakes through the tent, a colorful display of silk saris: scarlet, sapphire, emerald, violet. The young women's eyes are painted and their bodies perfumed. As they wind their way forward, they whisper among themselves, periodically erupting in nervous laughter.

To the left of Siddhartha's seat is a basket filled with ornate, engraved bangles of silver and gold, gifts from the head of the clan to his people. As each young woman approaches, she offers a delicate bow. Siddhartha takes her hand and slips a bracelet over her wrist onto her brown arm. The young women keep their eyes averted beneath headscarves, blushing, giggling, occasionally offering a shy smile. Siddhartha gazes at each one, taking them in with plaintive, searching eyes.

Yasodhara, the daughter of the king's sister, is the last in line. She is radiant, wearing a sari dyed a deep plum color. A sparkling ruby sets off the bronzed skin of her chiseled nose. Her thick hair is uncovered and falls across her shoulders in smooth waves, just as Maya's once did.

As she approaches the throne, I see Siddhartha's posture shift and his eyes brighten. When Yasodhara steps in front of him, she does not bow or look away. She keeps her spine upright and her head raised. She looks directly into his eyes.

"What do you have for me?" she asks, in a playful, teasing tone.

Siddhartha places the bag of bangles at his feet and removes a golden ring from his finger.

"This is for you," he says, placing the ring into the palm of her hand.

Yasodhara's full, painted lips part. She smiles at him, flashing a row of perfect white teeth. Then she turns and strolls away.

I watch him watching her. Yasodhara pauses and turns back, gazing at Siddhartha with a dazzling smile. He smiles in return. The energy between them is palpable and alive.

I see that he is smitten. I offer a plea to the gods: may this budding romance bring Siddhartha true happiness, ease his restless spirit, and tether him to the world.

Yasodhara married Prince Siddhartha and gave birth to their child, Rahula. Siddhartha abandoned Yasodhara when he departed the palace to pursue spiritual life. He left her without a man to legitimize her, and his family spurned her.

I wake up. A cold shudder passes through me. In a flash I realize he is gone. I cry out, waking the baby, who also begins to wail. Rahula and I are together. But now we are also alone.

Over the past months I have felt Siddhartha slipping away: moody, distracted, forlorn. Once just the sight of me was enough to bring him delight. But since the birth of Rahula, he has become more and more withdrawn. The joy disappeared from his eyes, replaced by deep sadness and discontent. He grew increasingly sullen, as if receding behind a wall of disappointment or regret.

During my pregnancy, I had a repeated dream: Siddhartha was drowning, tossed about in a moonlit, churning ocean. I would call out to him, extending my arms, reaching, and I'd watch with horror and dread as he sank beneath the surface of the dark, salty sea. Night after night I would wake with a start and reach for the warmth of him lying beside me. But many nights the bed was cold and empty. He was not there.

I would rouse myself and go to sit on the balcony, looking out across the palace gardens and the darkened hills beyond the palace. I sang quietly to myself and to the baby growing inside me, offering prayers for his safety and quick return; waiting impatiently until the clip-clop of hooves signaled his return; watching as he and his attendant, Channa, dismounted their horses.

I would rise and slip back into bed, pretending to be asleep, as he tip-toed into our quarters and slid under the covers beside me.

He never spoke of his journeys, and I never asked. But I sensed the secrets he carried churning inside him like gathering storm clouds. I watched rain and wind pass through him. I saw the lines of his face deepen and set. I heard his steps become labored and lose their lilt. I felt walls of impenetrable stone thicken around him.

The Shakya clan never fully welcomed me. I was always too loud, too bright, too independent. I spoke frequently and with passion, refusing to temper my emotions. I would not be submissive or silenced. And for this I was shunned, becoming an object of petty gossip among women of the court.

Siddhartha was my armor, my advocate, my protector. Without him by my side I will be scorned and reviled, an abandoned woman confined to his family home, left to raise our son without a father.

I pace the room, cradling Rahula in my arms, sobbing. He has left us. I cry until there are no more tears. Then my sadness turns to anger. Waves of fury and anguish rise from my belly. He promised to love and protect me. He lied! I was deceived, and now I am betrayed and abandoned.

I place the baby on the bed. I tear at my bedclothes, my hair, my skin. I stand alone, howling into the darkness.

The stories of these women are personal and universal. Passed down over generations, they are both factual accounts of individual people who lived, loved, and suffered, and archetypal facets of the universal feminine. As flesh-and-blood humans, their stories inform and inspire. As archetypal dimensions of humanity, they illuminate universal qualities we carry within us. Women and the feminine are alternately longed for, feared, despised, and ignored. But failing to integrate women's stories and feminine archetypes leads to an incomplete understanding of who we are. Without them, the fabric of our spiritual life remains frayed, torn, fractured.

Maya, the historical mother of the Buddha, tells the story of fullness and beauty. She is our inner royalty and elegance; the font of primal creativity and life; the womb from which all life comes. Like each of us, she is here and then gone.

Prajnaparamita is the perfection of wisdom, the ability to see the true nature of reality, which is personified as the mother of all Buddhas. She is timeless, boundless wisdom; the truth that transcends definition, duality, and words; fully embracing the moment; abiding at once nowhere and everywhere. *Prajnaparamita* is the eternal birthplace, ever present, unborn and undying.

We honor the son but neglect the source. We revere the blazing light of illumination that sees and knows and reveals, but not the dark mystery, unfathomable and unbound: the awesome force of the female body, stronger and more powerful than bows and arrows, guns or bombs. Feared, objectified, rejected.

Pajapati, the Buddha's aunt and foster mother, tells the story of compassion and the fearless, quivering heart. She is our warmth and tenderness; the intimate, tender sensitivity that feels everything and responds; the strength that embraces all of life with fierce, tenacious kindness.

Avalokitesvara, Quan Yin, and Tara are Buddhist icons that represent manifestations of compassion. They are bodhisattvas of tenderness and care who hear the cries of the world and reach out across distances and differences to listen, attend, and mend.

It is easy to mistake great compassion as being soft or fragile. But the compassionate heart is potent, resilient, robust, able to withstand the torrent of human pain and suffering without wilting, hardening, or defending. The etymological roots of the word *compassion* mean "to suffer with." Compassion is the heart that receives and responds, the heart that breaks open again and again, revealing our capacity to stretch, extend, and crack wide open, beyond what we imagined we could stand.

Yasodhara, the fiery, feisty wife, tells the story of the embodied feminine. She represents the energy of sexuality and passion. She is lust and anger, defiantly refusing to be cowed by convention. For this reason she is loathed, rejected, forsaken. But we deny her at great risk, for she is also the red thread of our vitality and life force. She is the vim and verve we carry inside us that calls out to be fully met.

This archetype appears in the form of wrathful *dakinis*—a Sanskrit term that describes the sharp, brilliant wisdom of the enlightened feminine, the raw energy of life itself. Wrathful *dakinis* represent the fierce force that will chop, slice, claw, and destroy any obstacle that threatens to obstruct the full expression of awakened life.

This flavor of the fierce feminine has been consistently denied a place in spiritual life. The influence of patriarchal power has kept it confined and under wraps. More often than not it is hidden out of sight. When it is not hidden, it is denigrated or reviled. After Siddhartha left his wife and son and became the Buddha, the great spiritual sage is reputed to have chided an errant monk by saying, "It is better to place your penis in the mouth of a poisonous cobra or in a bed of hot coals than to place it in the vagina of a woman."

But if, as Izumi Shikibu suggests, awakening is the realization of an embodied wholeness, then the historical voices of the women in the Buddha's life, as well as the archetypal feminine energies they represent—word-less wisdom and mystery, tender and fierce compassion, and wrath, passion, and sexuality—must be stitched back into the story.

In this way, walking the spiritual path becomes a process of personal integration as well as collective transformation, remembering and reweaving the neglected parts of our unique histories, and dismantling the gross and subtle inequities built into the misogynistic, patriarchal structures of spiritual institutions. Only by weaving the parts left out back into our individual and collective stories can we reclaim the full potential of what it means to be fully human.

11

ALL HANDS ON THE RIM

To integrate the feminine requires debunking the myth of the individual who succeeds based on their own solitary effort. There is no such thing. Personal success is not a solo act. It includes the social and economic circumstances an individual is born into and the opportunities those circumstances afford or deny.

To acknowledge this means to become aware of the many ways in which dominant culture wields power over nondominant groups—women, people of color, immigrants, those who are gender nonconforming, the LGBTQI community, and others. It means recognizing the inequitable distribution of wealth, land, and other resources that create an uneven playing field. It means telling the truth about how America and other imperialist nations were born of the genocide of native peoples and built on the backs of people who were enslaved. And it means coming to understand how these truths continue to maintain systems of privilege, perpetuate harm and violence, and cause profound disconnection and isolation.

At the heart of the bodhisattva is the understanding that personal awakening is inadequate and incomplete when others continue to suffer. It is only by revealing and reckoning with both individual *and* collective karma, dismantling personal ignorance and confusion *and* discriminatory systems of power and privilege, that real freedom is possible. Individual spiritual development requires seeing through the habitual belief in a solid, separate self. Collective spiritual development requires the courage and compassion to challenge hierarchical systems of inequity and to generate new forms of practice that honor the body and heart.

We cannot do this alone. We must do it together.

In 1999, Jungian therapist, activist, and author Jean Shinoda Bolen wrote a book titled *The Millionth Circle.* Her aim was to provide a model for women's Circles—a spiritual descendant of the consciousness-raising groups of the sixties and seventies—that would "inspire a worldwide healing force by bringing feminine values of relationship, nurturing, equality, cooperation, and interdependence into global culture." The idea is that as more and more women form and participate in these Circles, they will begin to change the culture, until we reach the metaphorical tipping point of the "millionth Circle" that will spark an evolution in human consciousness. In 2001 Shinoda Bolen collaborated with other women to form a Millionth Circle organization that does ongoing work to help realize this shift in awareness.

The shape of a circle represents wholeness, equality, and cohesion. As a verb, "to circle" means to gather together around a shared point of interest. Circles are an ancient form of social interaction. For millennia, people have assembled together around the fire to cook and share food; to tell stories and pass on indigenous knowledge; and to pray, worship, and honor the cycles of the body and the earth.

Circles do not engage hierarchical leadership. The central principle guiding Circle gatherings is "all hands on the rim." Each person is expected to participate fully, and everyone is equally responsible for the functioning of the whole. A Circle is a holding space where every unique voice is heard and respected. This takes time. If speed, efficiency, and productivity are the norm, then "circling" may feel like a slow, inefficient waste of time.

Although a Circle and a wheel are both round, they are not the same. As a wheel turns, it generates momentum to move us forward. As a Circle deepens, it turns into a cauldron, a container where all the parts left out simmer together over the fire until they become true nourishment. This is how alchemy happens. This is how transformation takes root.

I learned about Circles firsthand from my friend Diane. She and I met while I was working at New Ventures West. I had been assigned as her mentor to get her up to speed as she learned to lead our two-day coaching course. It was an awkward arrangement.

I didn't know Diane well, but I did know she was a polished professional with an impressive resume. Although I had more experience teaching coaching, she had more experience period. She was older, smarter, and more business-savvy than I. In the years I spent meditating in the monastery, she was the head of global diversity at Levi Strauss.

Sitting across from her at a conference table at the coaching school, I felt like an imposter. Diane wore textured earth tones: an ivory silk shirt, pleated sage green trousers, a tweed jacket, and refined gold jewelry. Her soft, round face and wide brown eyes exuded thoughtfulness. I was nervous, excited, overfriendly.

"Welcome!" I said with a big smile. "I'm so glad we have this chance to work together."

"Me, too," she said, nodding slightly.

Two fat three-ring binders with leader's notes sat on the table between us. "Shall we dive in?" I asked, pulling my binder toward me and flipping it open.

Diane paused. "I want to say something before we start," she said.

I flipped my binder closed, sat back in my chair, and waited.

She began, "It's really important to me . . ." Diane paused and cleared her throat before continuing.

"If we are going to work together," she said, "I want you to promise me that you won't *not* give me feedback because I'm black."

"Oh, of course not!" I stammered. "I mean, of course I'll give you feedback." I was trying to reassure her, but the speed of my response and my flustered, overeager tone gave me away.

She held me in a forthright, no-nonsense gaze. "If you can't give me feedback because you are uncomfortable," she said, deliberately enunciating each word, "then I won't be able to improve or grow."

I let her words sink in. With a long exhale I released the tightness in my belly. I ran the palms of my hands down the fronts of my arms to calm the anxiety buzzing just beneath the surface of my skin.

We locked eyes and took each other in. I felt her honesty and resolve puncture the stiff shell of my nervous politeness. Something between us softened and opened.

"I promise," I said slowly.

Diane's face broke into a grin, her eyes gleaming.

I grinned back. In that moment, the seeds of our long friendship were planted.

Two years later, when Diane's email arrived in my inbox asking if I wanted to participate in a new women's Circle, I didn't hesitate.

"I'm in!" I emailed back to her.

"It will be a mixed group, half black and half white," she explained, "with the aim of having real conversations about race and racism."

There were eight of us: me, Diane, Rachel, BZ, Sidalia, Emily, Barb, and Stacy—an economist, two executives, a financial planner, several coaches and consultants, and a musician. Many of the women had devoted their careers to creating equity and inclusion inside organizations. We were a group of movers and shakers. But we decided to do something surprising. Instead of jumping into action or taking up a project or cause, we declared that we would spend our time together solely building relationships. To help us remember, we named ourselves the IDK ("I Don't Know") Sisters.

True to Circle form, there was no leader. Each month we rotated our meeting to a different member's home. Our motto was, "You don't really know someone until you've eaten in their kitchen and peed in their toilet!"

At each meeting we lit a candle, did a short meditation, and shared about ourselves, our lives, and the impact of living in a racist country and culture. Sometimes we watched a video or shared a reading; sometimes we dove into heated discussion about racism in current events.

In time I came to see the original mix of four white and four black women with greater texture and shades of gray. Peeling back the layers, the full diversity and complexity of the group was revealed. Two white women were Jewish, and two others—one Greek and one from the Deep South—were a married couple, with two adopted black children. Two black women were married to black men; one was in a long-term partnership with a black woman; and the youngest was biracial, queer, and single.

Over the years, we shared promotions, job losses, and retirements, marriages and divorces, shootings and incarcerations, births and deaths. We cheered and wept together watching Obama's first election results pour in. We offered each other rides, brought each other meals, listened, gave hugs, and provided advice and consultation. On more than one occasion, we almost disbanded. But each time, one of us would place her hands firmly on the rim and pull us back together again.

Before IDK, I could hold the horrifying headlines, statistics, and stories I heard—about black and brown people followed in stores, mistreated by doctors, pulled over by cops, shot, beaten, or jailed—at a distance. But after hours of sitting in Circle listening to my IDK sisters, the same headlines and stories were no longer anonymous tragedies. They were stories about the families and loved ones of people I loved.

Still, I was slow to fully metabolize the reality of systemic inequity. I was unwilling to cop to the fact that, no matter how much I loved these women, we lived in fundamentally different worlds. My life was full of privilege, while theirs were shot through with relentless fear and danger I could choose to hear and see and feel—or not.

It took an even wider Circle for me to let this in.

After we had been meeting for a decade, IDK was invited to join a group of other women's Circles for a four-day retreat. There were thirty of us—women ages thirty to eighty from across the United States, spanning multiple ethnicities, religions, and sexual and gender identities. I volunteered to be on the Hub, the organizing committee for the event, which included myself; Stephanie, a white woman; and the indomitable Ronita, a black woman and author, artist, and activist who was one of the original founders of the Millionth Circle and had spent years convening Circles across the globe.

Ronita shared her Circle wisdom with us in monthly calls during the eight months leading up to the retreat. Together we dreamed and planned, ultimately crafting an elaborate agenda that included guided meditations, reflective questions, facilitated exercises, delicious homemade meals, and plenty of time for socializing, walking on the beach, and dancing.

On the first evening of the retreat, Ronita guided us in a ritual in which each woman placed an object representing her race, culture, and heritage on a table in the center, transforming it into an altar. The next morning, we began by sitting around the altar in meditation. When I rang the bell to signal the end of the silence, Ronita nudged Stephanie and me to the front of the room. We welcomed everyone and then began to bullet-point our agenda onto a flip chart.

"Oh no, no, no!" said Cherri, a black woman with long dreadlocks whose jewelry shook and rattled as she spoke. Cherri was a lawyer, the executive director of the Alameda County Family Justice Center, and a nationally recognized leader in the field of domestic violence.

"I am not here to be in a training," Cherri declared. "Or to be led."

Stephanie and I looked at one another, unsure how to proceed.

"This is a Circle," Cherri continued, rocking back and forth as she spoke. "I want to be in a Circle."

Oh, right. Stephanie and I were both experienced facilitators. But this was not about facilitation. It was something completely different.

We looked over at Ronita, who nodded at us to return to our seats. After an uneasy pause, she said, "I suggest we start with a song."

People shuffled in their seats as she cued up her iPhone and speaker to the song "Black Lives Matter," by Pastor Chris Harris.

The thumping beat of the lyrics spilled into the room: "What's the world. (Beat, beat.) Coming to. (Beat, beat.) We're losing hope. (Beat, beat.) But I've got good news. (Beat, beat.)" As the refrain kicked in, we added our voices: "Black. Lives. Matter. Black. Lives. Matter." This was followed by the haunting voice of Eric Garner, the black man choked to death by police in Brooklyn, repeating: "I can't breathe! I can't breathe!" while the song's backup singers chanted: "Hands up, don't shoot! Hands up, don't shoot!"

Some women stood and clapped. Some closed their eyes and swayed. Others joined hands or embraced. I dropped my head in my hands and sobbed. When the music ended, Cherri let out a deep wail, giving voice to our shared heartache.

A long, reverent silence followed.

Finally, Ronita began again. "Okay, now we're ready to open the Circle. We are all wise women, but we forget the power that lies within us. Circle is an opportunity for fearless wisdom to be spoken out of silence from our hearts and spirits. Sitting together in the cauldron, we create a unity far greater than the sum of our individual parts."

Then, one by one, each person spoke.

I don't remember what I said. I do remember the silent tears that slid down my face hour after hour as I listened to the stories: one woman's brother pulled over by police, handcuffed, and slammed against the hood of his car for "driving while black"; another woman's mother, ignored as she stood on the side of the road waving for help in a white neighborhood; parents unable to rent property or secure loans; sons and daughters denied jobs. As I listened and wept, I began to see that these individual stories were the result of a collective reality of injustice, poverty, and oppression—invisible to me as a white person—that black people live all the time.

I felt pained and grateful to hear this unguarded, searing truth. Feeling my heart crack wide open, I cherished the rawness of that honest ache.

By the time we broke for dinner, tendrils of tenderness crisscrossed the space. We ate and laughed and danced and laughed some more. By the time we closed the weekend, I was equally shattered and uplifted, devastated and inspired. Yes, there was excruciating pain and anguish and sorrow. But there was also astonishing strength and courage and beauty.

There are three words in English that describe the emotional resonance between subject and object, self and other: *sympathy, empathy,* and *intimacy. Sympathy* holds the other person at arm's length, maintaining a superior position. In sympathy, we feel sorry for them, those unfortunate people over there, who are not like me. *Empathy* pulls us in closer. Empathic resonance allows others' pain to touch our own heart. We feel their pain. For most of us, the word *intimacy* suggests sexuality—a kind of body-to-body, skin-to-skin closeness. But in Zen, intimacy points to something different. It refers to the teaching of "suchness," attributed to the Zen monk Dongshan, who lived in Tang dynasty China. Suchness is a translation of the term *tathata*, the paradoxical singularity of difference and unity expressed as the intimacy and immediacy of now.

We have all had a taste of this, even if a fleeting one: the startling, naked, as-is-ness of reality that reveals itself when the familiar discursive mind quiets, the friction between self and other abates, and what remains is just one thing. This flavor of intimacy is an immersive experience—a complete inclusivity that opens us to seeing everything freshly and understanding who and what we are in an entirely new way.

In his poem, "The Song of the Jewel Mirror," Dongshan opens with the line: "The teaching of suchness has been intimately transmitted from east to west." This refers to the transmission of suchness to his disciples and his disciples' disciples, including Dogen-zenji, who carried the teaching from China to Japan, where it became the heart and hallmark of Soto Zen.

Transmission is not a cognitive event in which information is passed from one mind to another. It's deeper and more intimate than that. Transmission is the joining of hearts, two people meeting unencumbered by past ideas, beliefs, and identities, allowing the vulnerability of not-knowing to birth something alive and true. It is an enigmatic experience beyond what words can convey.

This kind of transmission is also what happens in Circle. Individual selves enter, each carrying their unique flavor of pain and confusion. But as we sit together and listen, taking in others' stories and allowing them to pierce our defenses and identities, alchemy happens. Simmering together in the cauldron, the hard edges of our separation soften, and we discover a collective wholeness.

For me, taking in the pain and strength and beauty of others tore me open in ways I could not have imagined. Many times I thought, *I can't bear this. It's too much.* And perhaps it was too much for me alone. But it wasn't too much for all of us together.

The crises we are facing—irreversible climate change, widespread hatred and violence, the growing assault on the truth—are overwhelming. Too big for any of us to hold alone, they call us to join hands and join hearts, to come together in new ways and discover responses we have not yet dared to dream.

12

BIRTHING A NEW PATH

We are seated on a stage in two comfy chairs angled to face one another. In between us is a coffee table spread with a beige table-cloth and set with a vase of pale peach delphiniums, two empty glasses, and a pitcher of ice water. Lines of water bead upon and spill down the sides of the pitcher, pooling in a damp circle on the tablecloth. There are sixteen hundred people seated in the auditorium, their faces shadowed under the darkened house lights. The spotlights above the stage create a circle of warm yellow glow around us, evoking a sense of intimacy.

He is the headliner, a neuropsychologist, author, and expert on meditation and brain science. His job is to explain and elucidate. I am the interlocutor, a Buddhist teacher, there to stir, challenge, question.

In his blue blazer, crisp button-down shirt, and brown loafers, he holds forth in scientific vernacular, describing the brain as an organ housed inside the skull—the squishy gray stuff between the ears whose sensitive web of lightning-fast neurons shape and are shaped by experience. He uses words and phrases like *hippocampus, cortisol, amygdala, negativity bias.*

I ask, "Is the brain the same as the mind?"

"Now that's a big question!" he says with a chuckle, eliciting laughter from the audience.

"Yes," I say, "but an important one."

"They aren't the same," he explains, "but the mind is what the brain does."

"Do you mean 'big mind,' as in consciousness, or 'small mind,' the thinking mind?

He smiles and nods, but doesn't answer.

"And what about the brain in the belly?" I say.

The idea of a "diaphragm brain" dates back to Homer in 700 BCE. Like the cranial brain, the abdomen contains a complex of neurons complementary to the dense neuronal structure in the head. But rather than remaining enclosed within the skull, this enteric brain suffuses the entire viscera of the body. Whereas the neocortex of the cranial brain favors analysis, reason, abstract thinking, and logic, the enteric brain is intuitive, sensate, and holistic.

The concept of the belly as a seat of intelligence has arisen repeatedly over centuries, but each time, it has eventually been forgotten, brushed aside, ignored. In raising the idea now, I expect the same treatment. My conversation partner obliges.

"Here's how the brain works," he explains. "We are wired for survival. The baseline resting state of the brain is always tracking for danger. When we encounter a scary or difficult experience, or even imagine one, the amygdala sounds an alarm, causing the brain to release a cascade of chemicals—norepinephrine, adrenaline, cortisol—that prime us for 'fight or flight.'"

I understand that this is the current view of how we are wired. During the years I spent tending to Eugene, a wave of secular mindfulness—infused with scientific language, logic, and proof—spread through corporate America. At the time of my onstage conversation with the neuropsychologist, mindfulness had become a popular tool for rewiring neural pathways, increasing efficiency, and reducing stress. Based on my years of teaching PEP, I know the benefits of bringing meditative principles and practices into the workplace. But I am also wary of reducing the impact of mindfulness to a list of chemical reactions, and I'm reluctant to swap measurable scientific data for the beauty and mystery of the body-mind.

Science is the prevailing narrative of our time. It traffics in the language of absolute truth, establishing a tyranny of quantifiable outcomes and objective facts. I have no doubt that science and technology have improved the health and well-being of humanity, including my own. When I was first diagnosed with diabetes, I gave myself shots of bovine insulin with fat needles several times a day. Forty years later, I wear a pump that continually delivers human insulin under my skin, along with a continuous glucose monitor that reads and registers my blood-sugar levels through an app on my iPhone. Amazing.

But I am also aware of the limitations of the scientific worldview. Scientific theories are approximations of the truth that change over time. When I was eleven, type 1 diabetes was understood to be a genetic condition. A decade later, I was told: nope, it is viral. More recently, type 1 diabetes is described as an autoimmune condition. So I carry a healthy dose of skepticism.

I vividly recall listening to the doctor in the trauma unit in Santa Rosa as he described what we were seeing in the MRI image of Eugene's damaged brain. He pointed to a spray of black dots at the top of the image. "This is the neocortex," he explained, "where our executive functioning happens—how we make decisions, manage time, control emotions, focus, and multitask." The black dots were the places where blood had splattered across Eugene's squishy gray matter, compromising his ability to assess, decide, plan, remember. "Sometimes the blood is reabsorbed by the brain," the doctor told us, "but not always."

No one expected Eugene to fully recover. Several months after we left the hospital, one of the speech therapists from the brain rehab unit came to visit us at home. She was astonished at how well he was doing. "He's an outlier," she whispered to me as she left. "We never would have predicted this."

Science hypothesizes, maps, and predicts. But there are always outliers. No matter how complete scientific theories and explanations may be, there are always inexplicable parts of reality that remain outside the scope of what we know or can expect. Tests and measurements provide a baseline, but they fail to explain dimensions of reality outside the scope of what we can imagine.

"That's one explanation," I say to the neuropsychologist, doing my best to smooth the quaking in my voice. I take a long sip of cool water and place the damp glass back on the table between us. I don't want to pick a fight. But I also don't want to be silenced. This is not the first time I've taken on scientific authority and expertise. And when I've done it in the past, it did not go well.

As an undergraduate at Wesleyan University in the mid-1980s, I completed thesis work on the impact of science on the shape of Western medicine: how it emphasizes curing over healing and is biased toward treatment of acute conditions rather than chronic ones. I studied the work of Thomas Kuhn, whose revolutionary book *The Structure of Scientific Revolutions* poked holes in the notion of scientific progress as the straightforward accumulation of objective fact. He described the history of scientific theories as a series of paradigms that remain intact as long as they provide a relatively coherent map of reality. Eventually, however, as new data is unearthed, each paradigm begins to fray and unravel. One story gives way to another, as happened in the transition between Newtonian physics and quantum physics.

Kuhn's work underscores the notion that context is as important as content, meaning that objective facts are shaped by subjective orientation and bias. What we see and know is determined by where we look, what we pay attention to—and what we don't. Facts that confirm the current paradigm are highlighted and underscored, while those that challenge it are ignored, forgotten, or brushed aside.

After the publication of his book, Kuhn found himself on the receiving end of disparagement and ire from the scientific community. In my final year at Wesleyan, I did, too. In defense of my thesis, I participated in oral exams in which three white men seated behind a long oak table—a biochemist, a microbiologist, and a nuclear physicist—tapped their pens on the table as they peppered me with questions.

"Miss Weiss appears to be an intelligent young woman," they wrote in their review of me. "We sincerely hope she takes time to learn something about science."

I was outraged then, and the heat of my anger bubbles up once again as Blue Blazer continues to hold forth. His simple, clear explanations echo current neuroscientific understanding and offer bite-sized morsels for the audience to help relieve the stress and distress of our fast-paced, wired, 24-7 culture. They are useful and well-intentioned. But they are only half true.

The term "survival of the fittest" is mistakenly attributed to Charles Darwin in his book *Descent of Man*. The term was actually not Darwin's at all but was coined by Herbert Spencer and promotes the fierce, do-or-die competition needed to support a capitalist system. Spencer became the leading advocate of "social Darwinism" and the eugenics movement, which misused Darwin's scientific observations to justify the racist, misogynist doctrine that "the strong should stay strong and the weak should stay weak, for it is their nature."

This misappropriation of science to justify the oppression of those who are not in power has reared its head repeatedly over the decades—as the forced sterilization of the "feebleminded" and of black people in America, and as Hitler's extermination of Jews, homosexuals, and Roma people during World War II.

A lesser-known term, from Darwin's *The Expression of Emotion in Man and Animals,* establishes that expression of empathy is universal among mammals, suggesting that our survival is less about competition than it is about collaboration. Yet "survival of the fittest" became the soundbite on Darwin, while his theory of "survival of the kindest" is barely known and rarely cited.

The use of the term "fight or flight" follows a similar trajectory. It was coined by Harvard psychologist Walter Bradford Cannon. In his 1932 book *The Wisdom of the Body,* he describes how stress affects the sympathetic nervous system by causing the pituitary gland to secrete ACTH, resulting in the activation of the amygdala and hypothalamus and causing a sharp rise in cortisol—just as my friend in the blue blazer explained to the audience.

But a study conducted by Shelley Taylor at UCLA in 2001 reveals a decidedly different stress response in female rats and humans. Instead of a cortisol-driven "fight or flight" response, females are more likely to respond with the secretion of oxytocin, which produces conduct described as "tend and befriend." Instead of aggression or fear, females exhibit behavior that nurtures and connects.

Community, connection, and mutual support are an equally valid set of behaviors for managing stress. So why do "survival of the fittest" and "fight or flight" remain central to the modern scientific lexicon, while "survival of the kindest" and "tend and befriend" are consistently overlooked and ignored? Content and context must be examined together.

Sitting onstage, I am reluctant to discuss the history of misogyny that underlies the current scientific data. I tell myself that people came to hear what he has to say. The information he's providing is practical, tactical, useful. If I speak up, maybe they will hate me or boo me off stage.

I am acutely aware of the names given to women who refuse to bow to patriarchal authority: *dragon lady, temptress, evil stepmother, bitch*. But I cannot hold my tongue. The weight of centuries of suppression and silence bears down on me. So I speak.

I recite from memory, summoning the words of Dogen-zenji, the thirteenth-century Zen philosopher-poet-monk: "When you sail out in a boat to the middle of the ocean where no land is in sight and view the four directions, the ocean looks circular and does not look any other way. But the ocean is neither round or square," I say, my voice rising. "Its features are infinite in variety. It is like a palace, it is like a jewel. It only looks circular as far as the eye can see at this time. All things are like this."

"Lovely!" he says, as he places his notes on the table. "Maybe that's a good place to stop and take some questions."

The house lights go up, and I peer out into a sea of faces. Hands are raised; runners appear with microphones. I don't remember every question, but I do remember their tone. There is a palpable ache in the inquiries. Like me, the people in the audience want to make sense of their struggles and pain. They are looking to the expert in a blue blazer for an answer, a fix, a cure. Like me, they are seeking wise counsel from outside to ease their distress, their hurt, their heartache. He answers with sincerity and genuine warmth. His explanations bring the promise of relief, offering theories and practices to rewire the circuitry in the brain.

My mind drifts as I listen. I want to know how things work too. But not at the expense of wonder. I want a framework big enough to hold the fullness of our complexity and curiosity. I want to erase the sharp lines of certitude, to step outside of sureness into the wide, wild mystery of things.

The Chinese character for "human" is a stick figure, stretched between heaven and earth, between our infinite potential and our gritty limitations. We live in two dimensions: the horizontal and the vertical. The horizontal plane is about moving across the surfaces, getting from here to there. It's about being productive, getting stuff done. In the horizontal plane, speed and efficiency reign.

Getting stuff done is good. I love crossing things off my to-do list. The trouble is, there is always more to do: more dishes to wash, more email to answer, more rungs on the ladder, more gold rings to chase. Buddhist teaching refers to this phenomenon as the Wheel of Samsara—the perpetual cycle of turning and churning, beginningless and endless. When we live only in the horizontal dimension, we are hamsters running on a wheel. Round and round we go, driven to reach an imaginary finish line that's always just around the bend.

The vertical plane invites us to sink beneath the surface, into our depths; it is about being fully present for what is happening each moment. Dropping into the vertical, we descend into the bottomless *now*. We shift from what the ancient Greeks called *chronos*—linear, sequential, tick-tock time—into *kairos*, the timeless moment. We experience this when time becomes fluid and moments slow and open, or speed by in a flash. Or when we are swept away by the beauty of the sky, or the body, or a work of art. Or when we are immersed in intimate conversation and discover that in what felt like minutes, hours have passed.

Without the horizontal, we may fail to tap the potential for manifestation and expression. But without the vertical, we risk living in meaningless efficiency.

Integrating the vertical dimension of *kairos* demands shifting from linear, fact-based *logos* (logic) to poetic, anecdotal *muthos* (story or myth.) As the feminist poet Muriel Rukeyser wrote: "The universe is made of stories, not of atoms." And stories are more than just a reporting of facts. To use novelist E.M. Forster's famous example, the sentence "The king died and then the queen died" is simple reporting. The sentence "The king died and then the queen died of grief" adds the affective richness of story.

The language of story does not merely describe; a well-crafted story provides a framework for understanding where we came from, where we are, and where we are going. The stories we inhabit bring a fullness to our experience that helps reveal intention, impact, and alchemy. Our stories link the personal and the universal, the mundane and the numinous.

Homo sapiens sapiens is the Latin term for the human species. The double *sapiens* points to our unique capacity for self-reflection, our ability to know that we know. We are a species of storytellers and meaning-makers. We weave worlds with words.

Each of us lives inside an individual narrative. What we think and say and do is shaped by our past. The family whose norms we followed or rebelled against, our ethnicity and race, our gender identity, sexuality, and economic status are all threads in the tapestry we become. Those influences become a set of lenses we look through, coloring how we see and relate to ourselves and others and how we make sense of the world. The personal narrative we embody largely determines what we value and what we ignore or discard.

As Anaïs Nin memorably wrote, "We don't see the world as it is, we see it as we are." But we also live inside a collective narrative, a set of cultural assumptions that shape our institutions, systems, and structures. Shared cultural narratives overlap and intersect with the personal, but shared narratives can be hazy and hard to see. They show up as unspoken conventions and implicit bias—prejudice and preferences of which we are unaware of and that many of us would be unwilling to admit.

Few people would say out loud that women are less capable leaders than men, that white job applicants should be chosen over black applicants, or that black people feel less pain than whites. Yet research studies show consistent patterns of discrimination and disparity based on gender and race. White women continue to lag behind men in leadership positions, while women of color lag further still. Applicants with "white-sounding" names get about 50 percent more job call-backs than applicants with "black-sounding" names on otherwise identical resumes. Physicians routinely recommend less pain medication for black patients than for white patients with the same injury or condition.

Implicit bias is not the consequence of individual psychology. It is a collective, social phenomenon. Just as our personal perspective shapes how we know and engage the world, collective cultural attitudes shape how we feel about and experience ourselves and each other. Although implicit bias is unconscious, it has a profound impact on individual and collective perceptions and behavior.

While I was living at Tassajara, I spent several winters immersed in studying the *Vijnaptimatradasidi*, written by Vasubandhu, the fourth-century Buddhist philosopher best known as the father of Buddhist psychology. In this ancient, esoteric text, Vasubandhu offers an explanation of how habits function and how implicit bias works. He explains that below the level of our conscious awareness, every moment of experience plants a "seed" in the flowing river of *alaya*, or "storehouse" consciousness. These seeds, which shape how we perceive the world, bear "fruit" as our ideas, beliefs, and actions. In other words, we never see the world through clear, unfiltered lenses; we see it through lenses colored by both our personal, psychological history and by the ubiquitous cultural waters in which we swim.

When we understand that this process is built into the fundamental structure of human consciousness, it takes the bite out of bias. Instead of blaming or shaming or trying to convince ourselves (and others) it isn't true, we can assume that bias is always present and begin to wake up to how it functions. If we know that what we know is always partial, it allows us to swap rigidity, righteousness, and dogma for openness, interest, and curiosity.

Several days after the event on stage, I begin receiving hate email—from women. "You were disrespectful, shrill, out of place." "My friends and I spent the whole ride home talking about how angry and rude you were." As I read, I feel the same quaking I felt before I spoke. I want to scream at the computer screen or throw it across the room. Instead, I close the computer and go for a swim, kicking out my frustration and hurt as I glide through the water.

Afterward, standing under a spray of warm water in the shower, I hear the words under their words: How. Dare. You. How dare you refuse to bow to male authority. How dare you not be nice. How dare you not accommodate, flatter, praise. How dare you speak your mind. How dare you speak at all.

Susan B. Anthony, the nineteenth-century antislavery activist and leader of the women's suffrage movement in the United States, would not have been surprised. She writes: "No advanced step taken by women has been so bitterly contested as that of speaking in public." Which is exactly what I have done.

Writer, historian, and social critic Rebecca Solnit makes a distinction between quiet and silence in her book *The Mother of All Questions,* in a brilliant chapter titled "A Short History of Silences." Being quiet is something we seek. Being silenced is something imposed upon us. She paints a clear picture of the fast-moving trajectory from the silencing of women into discrimination, oppression, violence, and death.

The Equal Rights Amendment to the US Constitution, which would guarantee equal rights to all Americans regardless of sex, was ratified by Congress in 1972 but has so far not been ratified by enough states to become law. Similarly, although the Equal Pay Act passed many decades ago, white women still make 79 cents to the dollar compared with men, and the pay gap for women of color is much wider: Latina women make 58 percent of men's earnings, and African American women make 65 percent.

It's easy to read these statistics as mere numbers, but they are more than that. They reflect the quality of women's lives, the power they (do not) hold, and their inability to have a voice, make an impact, or live to the fullest of their potential. And it gets worse.

Economic gender bias quickly bleeds into violence. The World Health Organization reports that one in three women experiences physical and/or sexual violence from an intimate partner. In the United States, one in five women will be raped in her lifetime. This amounts to one rape reported in the US every 6.2 minutes. Because the likelihood of conviction is painfully low and the consequences for women who come forward to report being raped are frequently devastating, it is well documented that the true number of rapes and assaults is at least five times that high.

This long history of violence and oppression plays out on women's bodies. But it hurts everyone. People of all genders are affected because when any one of us suffers, we all suffer. As author and social activist bell hooks writes, "The first act of violence patriarchy demands of males is not violence toward women. Instead, patriarchy demands of all males that they engage in acts of psychic self-mutilation, that they kill off the emotional parts of themselves."

Research shows what early-childhood teachers have always known: from infancy through age four or five, boys are more emotive than girls, but their feelings and vulnerability get socialized out of them. By the time most boys reach adolescence they have established a rubbery layer of pseudo-tough-guy independence and invincibility. For those who go on to college, they encounter what has come to be called the "bro code": hard drinking and partying paired with respect from other "bros" in direct proportion to their disrespect toward women.

Basketball player and five-time NBA All-Star Kevin Love shared an intimate exposé of the cost of the bro code in his life in a March 6, 2018, article on the sports website *The Players' Tribune*. He writes: "Growing up, you figure out really quickly how a boy is supposed to act. You learn what it takes to 'be a man.' It's like a playbook: Be strong. Don't talk about your feelings. Get through it on your own.... These values about men and toughness are so ordinary that they're everywhere, and invisible at the same time, surrounding us like air or water." This was a remarkable move from a twenty-nine-year-old superstar.

It's hard to see the cultural water we swim in. For Love it took a panic attack on court to make him stop, step back, and begin to unravel the invisible assumptions he was living in. But perhaps most interestingly, he says that as difficult as it was to navigate his panic, the most difficult part came afterward: "I'd thought the hardest part was over after I had the panic attack. It was the opposite. Now I was left wondering why it happened—and why I didn't want to talk about it."

Take that in for a moment: for Love, surviving a panic attack was not nearly as hard as it was to tell people about it. He explains: "I didn't want people to perceive me as somehow less reliable as a teammate, and it all went back to the playbook I'd learned growing up. All of us live inside an (often invisible) playbook; a set of culturally determined norms and assumptions that shape who we are and what we imagine is possible."

Speaking up is the first step toward untangling the tangle of unseen rules and conventions that tie us up in knots. Like pulling off a bandage, it may hurt. But as the early AIDS activists knew well: silence = death.

———

When I get home from my swim, it is clear that, again, I need to speak. I call Blue Blazer and tell him about the emails I received. I read them to him, letting the intensity of the words reverberate in the space between us. Then I listen to his silence on the other end of the line.

"I know we disagreed," I say, "and I acknowledge that I felt frustrated at points in our conversation, but I hope you didn't feel that I was abrasive or unkind."

I wait for a response. When nothing comes, I say, "If I said anything that felt disrespectful, I apologize."

"Oh no!" he says. "I'm so glad you called." A wave of relief washes through me.

"That was not my experience at all," he continues. "In fact, I was just singing your praises to my wife, telling her how much I appreciated your clarity and keen observation."

"I'm so glad," I say.

"Your role was to be provocative. Without that, it would have been pretty dull," he says with a chuckle. "There has to be room for different opinions and points of view." Then he invites me to lead a class for his community.

I feel a surge of shame for the irritation and pettiness I have been harboring, and I'm humbled by how easily my chafing at systemic inequity allowed me to cast him in the role of "other": privileged white guy, without a clue. As I take in his generosity and largesse, I see it is possible to clang and clash without severing connection; to bend without breaking the threads of relationship.

After we hang up, I lie on the floor of my office, breathing. A few warm tears spill out of my eyes and roll down my cheeks. Only now do I feel the full impact of the stress and worry I've been carrying. I let the weight of my body soften and relax, allowing the density of my bones and muscles to be supported, held by the soft woolen carpet beneath me, and the floor, and the earth.

For many years, I only knew of the first part of Inanna's story—how she hears the cries of her sister, descends, dies, and rises again. But later, when I uncovered more of the Inanna myth, I was delighted to discover that the story reveals the process of maturing and integrating masculine and feminine into a robust, intact whole.

When Inanna ascends from the Underworld back to the world of the Great Above, she discovers her husband, Dumuzi, seated on her throne, dressed in lavish silk garments and being fed sumptuous food. She is not pleased. In her absence, the rain has ceased and a great drought has descended across the land. She returns to find crops dying, the rivers gone dry, and her people starving.

Inanna flies into a rage. She declares that Dumuzi must immediately be removed from the throne and must descend into the Underworld as her replacement. Banishing Dumuzi to the Underworld is the equivalent of calling for his death. Just as Ereshkigal killed Inanna when she arrived, Inanna now inflicts the same fate on her wayward spouse.

During a time of widespread distress, Dumuzi remained well dressed and well fed, untouched by the misery unfolding outside the walls of the palace. He did not call up the courage or conviction to step outside his life of comfort or lend a hand. This choice, to remain swaddled and protected, is exactly what the young Prince Siddhartha shunned. Instead of remaining sheltered within the palace walls, he gave up his life of ease and devoted himself to ending human anguish—not just for himself but for everyone, everywhere.

Remember: this is myth, not history. Like dreams, myths unfold in images and archetypes, not facts. We can understand each character in a mythic story as an aspect of our own psyche. Inanna's sister, Ereshkigal, represents the submerged parts of herself that have gone unseen and untended. Her death at the hands of Ereshkigal causes Inanna to fully embody the suffering of her own undigested sorrow and grief, and she returns home a more mature version of her younger self.

When Inanna encounters Dumuzi, the insensitive man-child who has stolen her seat, she banishes her inner adolescent masculine, allowing herself to step into her own authority. The immature masculine displays itself as a narcissistic bully—an ignorant, pampered, unfeeling person who cannot relate to others in a generous, caring way. By exiling these characteristics, Innana sets herself up to rule as a strong, compassionate leader.

These two dimensions of Inanna's story represent the "yes" and "no" dimensions of the spiritual journey. The "yes" side of the journey is about inclusion, stitching the ignored and excluded threads of the psyche back into wholeness. The "no" side of the journey is about using one's power to vanquish ignorance and harm. When Inanna departs into the Underworld, what is demanded of her is letting go, complete surrender. But when she returns, what is needed is fierce clarity and strength. Here she is asked to step up and step in, wielding her power to jettison the privileged masculine. Inanna must interweave her willingness to yield and capitulate with the full force of her fury. Her tender, wholehearted "yes" must be balanced with a potent, unwavering "no."

Something similar occurs when the newly awakened Buddha returns to visit his family home. He is welcomed with open arms by his father,

Suddhodana, and his foster mother, Pajapati. But Yasodhara, the wife and young mother he abandoned, is enraged. She refuses to see him. Where the others greet the Buddha with a wholehearted "yes," Yasodhara responds with a clear, uncompromising "no."

It is easy to dismiss Yasodhara's anger and lack of forgiveness as a flaw, clear evidence of her lack of spiritual maturity. But we can also understand her response as arising from the willingness to embrace and embody her anger instead of denying or rejecting it or tucking it away. Rather than a limitation or weakness, we can see Yasodhara's anger and courage to voice a fierce "no" as a hard-won capacity, not as a failing. Yasodhara's "no" is a clear articulation that something is amiss and that the feminine has been denied an equal place within the Buddha's teachings and community.

Yasodhara's anger is a sharp reminder that her role—of wife, lover, parent, tender of the hearth—is consistently left out of the spiritual narrative. By giving it voice, she points to the need for adapting forms that fully embrace both masculine and feminine, monk and householder, holy and mundane as equally valid facets of human and spiritual life.

Many attempts have been made over the millennia to address the awkward problem of Yasodhara. In the early versions of the teachings recorded in the Pali Canon, she remains a side note, parenthetical to the main story, barely worth more than a few meager sentences. In these accounts of the narrative, she is nearly nonexistent, hovering around the edges of the texts like a ghost or a whisper. In some instances she is not even referred to by her name but is described as "the mother of Rahula."

The teachings in the Pali Canon were recorded years after the Buddha's death to preserve the purity and sanctity of Buddhist principles and teachings. The Buddha intentionally offered his teachings in Pali, the common language of the people, rather than Sanskrit, the older, more liturgical language. Yet very little detail about Siddhartha's personal, cultural, or family life appears in the Canon. Each section of the Canon, called a *sutta* in Pali, opens with the phrase, "Thus have I heard." The Canon is understood to contain the true spoken words of the Buddha as remembered by his attendant, Ananda. But the *suttas* present virtually no biographical details from the Buddha's life; "just the facts" are written down, with little context about the man who embodied them or the world he inhabited.

Later personal and biographical stories about the Buddha captured by subsequent schools of Buddhism portray colorful details and interpretations of Siddhartha's life prior to his enlightenment, including stories of how he met, fell in love with, and married his wife. In some accounts, after Siddhartha leaves, Yasodhara enters a parallel period of ascetic practices, shaving her head and wearing robes. Most accounts say that, like their son, Rahula, who becomes a Buddhist monk, she, too, eventually becomes a nun and joins his *sangha*.

A lesser-known version of the story (found within the Sarvastivada school, and given voice by Buddhist professor and author John Strong) tells that Yasodhara and Siddhartha make love the night of his departure. After he leaves the palace, she remains pregnant for six years—the same six years as Siddhartha's period of asceticism and wandering. In this version of the story, Yasodhara gives birth to Rahula at precisely the moment of Siddhartha's awakening. Here, Yasodhara and Siddhartha travel parallel paths; not the same, but equally compelling and legitimate.

What if living a life of spiritual renunciation and living fully immersed in the world were understood as two different but equally valid and acceptable paths? What would it look like to reimagine and rescript the patriarchal rendering of the spiritual journey to include the feminine? What if Yasodhara's experience—giving birth, raising a child, tending the garden, caring for the hearth and the earth—was also a complete path toward freedom and peace?

Archetypal masculine and feminine energies are wider and more comprehensive than common definitions of male and female gender. These archetypes are not about gender identity; they represent universal forces— what Carl Jung called the *anima* (feminine) and *animus* (masculine)—that exist in each of us. Together they symbolize the dynamic interplay between yin and yang, dark and light, warm and cool, hard and soft, slow and fast, body and mind, penetrating and receptive, emotion and intellect, clarity and mystery, intuition and reason. When they are in balance, life flows with grace and ease. Good health and balance reign in our minds and bodies, and all across the planet. Winter turns to spring, summer turns to fall, and all is right in the world.

But when these energies fall out of balance, chaos descends. The delicate turning of the seasons tilts into tumultuous climate extremes, fear and divisiveness reign, sectarian dogma fills the airwaves, and episodes of violence escalate. The emergence of these issues today suggests the need for recalibration of our global governing structures and policies, and of the confusion embedded in our hearts and minds that keeps the wheel of human and planetary destruction and devastation turning.

We live in a time that is profoundly out of balance. If we look at our use of language, we can see how it reflects the ways in which we favor masculine qualities. Listen: hard, fast, light, cool, penetrating, mind, intellect, clarity, reason, transcendence. And: soft, slow, dark, warm, receptive, body, emotion, mystery, intuition, transformation. We champion the mind over the body, and we esteem mental clarity over messy, irrational feelings and intuition. We prefer fast over slow and hard over soft. We champion knowing, are uncomfortable with the unknown, and suspicious of the mysterious. We speak of "en-light-enment" as waking up from darkness and delusion.

Jung proposes that integrating the inner *anima* and *animus* is the fundamental task of being human. This is a two-way process that involves weaving qualities of the mature feminine—listening, nurturing, tenderness, and compassion—into the immature, insensitive, divide-and-conquer, ruthless masculine. It also involves weaving qualities of the mature masculine—clarity, rationality, strength, and decisiveness—into the tentative, irrational, overly accommodating feminine. In this way, we hone the capacity to both attend and extend, learning to attune to the suffering of others and to take clear and decisive action.

The mature feminine comes into wholeness by finding inner courage, expressing a clear, bold voice, and refusing to be pushed aside. This is Maha Pajapati, Siddhartha's foster mother, walking hundreds of miles on foot to petition the Buddha for entry into the community. And it is Inanna, feeling wrath toward her disrespectful, insensitive lover and expressing an uncompromising "no" to the man who tried to pilfer her power.

The mature masculine grows and develops by learning to quell the incessant need for attention and accomplishment, and by being willing to step out of the spotlight into the role of advocate or ally. This is Ananda, the Buddha's trusted attendant, who hears Pajapati's cries, feels the pain of her exclusion, and uses his privileged relationship with the Buddha to advocate on her behalf. It is Father Enki, who listens with a pained heart when he hears that Innana has not returned from the Underworld and who uses his authority and magic to help rescue her.

A model of masculine and feminine parity is needed to discover creativity, vitality, and balance. Each of us must metabolize our suffering by facing the truths of grief, loss, and loneliness that are part and parcel of every human life. When we do, we have the opportunity to mature and ripen. In this way, both the masculine and feminine grow up within us, regardless of our gender identity.

When Inanna removes Dumuzi from the throne, he flees into the wilds in an effort to escape being dragged down into the Underworld. After he leaves, Inanna finds herself forlorn, full of grief. She misses him. Here Inanna embodies the experience of loss and loneliness, assimilating the lessons she learned in the Underworld from Ereshkigal, who was also grieving the death of her spouse. In this part of the story, we witness the invincible goddess crashing down to earth and getting messy. This is where transcendence meets transformation, perfection meets limitation, and godliness meets human grit and tenderness.

Meanwhile, Dumuzi, the vanquished king, undergoes his own transformation. Seated on Inanna's throne, he was unable to feel his own vulnerability and had little compassion for the suffering of others. But now he is forced to confront his weakness and impotence. After being stripped of his crown, his role, and his virility, he flees, haggard and undone, across the steppes of the countryside, pursued by the terrifying *gala:* creatures from the Underworld who want to capture and drag him underground.

Dumuzi becomes an outcast and a refugee, moving from place to place, hiding in barns, haystacks, and animal pens, trying to evade his would-be captors. This goes on until one night he has a dream in which he meets his sister, Geshtinanna. In the dream, he pours out his fear and distress to her, and she listens tenderly. When he awakens, he seeks Geshtinanna out and recounts the dream to her. In desperation, he begs her to petition Inanna to call off the *gala*.

As Geshtinanna listens tenderly, her eyes fill with tears and her heart swells with compassion. She leaves her brother and travels to Inanna's palace to speak with her. There, she describes her brother's misery and begs Inanna to remove the curse of the *gala* and take him back. Dumuzi has changed, she tells Inanna. He has faced his own grief, fear, and vulnerability, and he has become wiser, softer, and humbler for it. Inanna, moved by Geshtinanna's words, agrees to take Dumuzi back and return him to his role as her husband and consort.

But there is a catch. Not everyone can remain in the Great Above. *Someone* must return with the *gala* to the Great Below. Who will go with them?

A compromise is reached. The brother-and-sister team of Dumuzi and Geshtinanna agree to share the task. For half the year Dumuzi will live above ground with Inanna. During this time, sunshine and rain will fall, the rivers will flow, fruit and flowers will bloom, and the crops in the fields will ripen. In the other half of the year, Dumuzi will descend into the Underworld, surrendering into a period of inactivity, reflection, and stillness. And the reverse will be true for Geshtinanna: while Dumuzi lives above ground, she will go under, and while Dumuzi goes into the Underworld, she will resurface. In this way, the archetypal brother-and-sister team balance one another, honoring both masculine and feminine, light and dark, activity and stillness, above and below.

This model of masculine and feminine parity offers an example of authentic integration, not as uniformity, but as wholeness. True equality does not mean we become the same or even similar. Wholeness is not homogeneity. It is the full appreciation and celebration of differences. Winter is winter. Spring is spring. Maturity means appreciating both the unspoiled beauty of snowfall and the roaring yellow bloom of tulips.

We live in complex, divisive times. Our wide, aching world is calling out for integrated, innovative forms of spiritual life and practice to meet the potent challenges we face: climate change, growing economic disparity, and entrenched systems of racism, misogyny, and oppression. Science and technology may help to solve some of these problems, but the ability to transform hearts and minds demands more than just chemical or technical change. As Proust once said: "The real journey of discovery, is not to travel to new lands, but to see with new eyes."

The world is calling us to give birth to new norms. This task requires us to embrace paradox and mystery and to give ourselves over to the beautiful, terrifying unknown. This takes courage and compassion, wisdom and generosity, and the ongoing willingness to listen deeply and to speak our truth.

Only together can we see the entire sky.

EPILOGUE

Almost thirty years after leaving the San Francisco Zen Center, I sat with Teah in the hot tub at the Jewish Community Center after a swim with muscles stretched and aerated, and goggle marks imprinted in lumpy circles around our eyes. This is a ritual we've repeated multiple times each week, week after week for years. Teah spends half the year living as a Zen priest in San Francisco and the other half as the head teacher of the Brooklyn Zen Center. She is like a big sister to me, and we share an endearment and intimacy that belie the nearly twenty years between us.

We first met at Tassajara during the summer of 1987: two short Jewish women cranking wrenches, smearing grease, and laughing in the auto shop as we figured out how to replace the brake pads on my old Honda. Later, splayed across a foam futon in the heart of the winter, we studied Nagarjuna and Vasubandhu in the kerosene-lamp-lit woodstove warmth of her yurt, infusing old words with living meaning conjured from the fresh concerns of our current monastic life.

When I became a captive caregiver at Eugene's bedside in the ICU in Santa Rosa, Teah brought me a suitcase holding jeans, sweaters, and warm socks. I stood by her side when a cranky adversary at the San Francisco Zen Center lodged a formal complaint against her. We shared cramped hands and creaky knees, blisters and blustery winds, pedaling hundreds of miles on the AIDS Ride from San Francisco to LA, peals of laughter erupting as we hobbled to our room in a Hollywood hotel with spent muscles and bottomless hunger, devouring a burger and fries, fish tacos, and an ice cream sundae with nuts and whipped cream on top.

Our recent adventures have become more subdued: meeting at the local pool to swim and soak. I arrive at the pool, lugging my gym bag over my shoulder as I climb the stairs from the parking garage, and I see Teah seated on the bench in the lobby, plugged into her iPhone. She looks up and sees me. Her eyes brighten. I smile. Here we are again.

We descend into the locker room, undress, pull on our swimsuits, and head to the pool to kick out laps. Then afterward, a delicious soak in the tub. Foaming hot water softens and cajoles as we launch into familiar topics: her son, my blood sugar, how to work with a student who is stuck.

For many months Teah has gently batted a question my way: would you complete your training by going through dharma transmission? Dharma transmission is an elaborate, esoteric Zen ritual in which an authorized teacher recognizes the maturity and understanding of a student and empowers them to pass on the lineage to others. It is a mysterious, nonlinear process that has been passed down for hundreds of years, an intimate meeting where the essence of the teachings flow from one warm heart into another.

When I left the San Francisco Zen center, I tucked the possibility of receiving dharma transmission away. Over the years, when I observed friends and colleagues complete the process, I wondered about the path I had not taken. I wondered what might have happened if I had stayed and ordained. I wondered how my life might have unfolded if there had been a wider opening for me to step through, a point of entry broad enough to accommodate my choices and my life as a devoted practitioner living in the world.

But at that time, there was no doorway. Each time a pang of disappointment arose in me, I set it aside. *I made my choices and have no regrets,* I told myself, until little by little what had been a fierce longing became a dull ache.

Each time Teah asked me about transmission, I said, "I'm busy," or "I'm teaching in a different lineage now," or "It has been years since I have actively practiced in Zen."

But she is not dissuaded. "I have watched you closely over the years," she says, "and I have no doubt that you are truly a Zen teacher."

Then one afternoon as we soak in the tub, she asks again, and before I have a chance to reason or defend, I hear a robust, heartfelt confirmation spill out of me. "Yes," I say. "Yes, I will."

As soon as I hear my words, I know they are true. We lock eyes and fall silent. I feel surprised, delighted, and utterly sure. Now I understand that her request is an invitation—a new doorway I must step through without knowing what is on the other side.

Sixteen months later I take that step.

Dharma transmission is a seven-day ceremony, Zen at its refined, esoteric, essential best. The scent of incense. The deep resonance of the bell. The swish of elegant robes. Each day is filled with dozens of bows: full prostrations for each name on the twenty-six-hundred-year-old bloodline. Every morning I bow to the names of the men who walked the path before me. Every afternoon I bow to the names of women. With each prostration I bend the full length of my body down to the floor, press my forehead into the cool of the floorboards, and lift my hands skyward in a gesture of surrender and gratefulness. After hundreds of bows, the days blur. My back aches, my knees swell like melons, and my typical clear thinking turns vague and soft around the edges.

Between rounds of bowing, I stand arched over long swathes of starched white silk, painting the names of ancestors in fresh, black sumi ink, prepared by grinding an inkstick and water across the surface of an ink stone to get the consistency just right. Too thin and the letters bleed and blur across the fabric; too thick and the ink gums the fine bristles of the brush and sits on top of the silk in little blobs.

Each name carries the story of a life devoted to awakening, a heart and mind dedicated to untangling human suffering and angst. The names weave a singular tapestry of nascent love matured by work and wisdom across diverse time and place, culture and language. Name by name I inscribe myself into the lineage. Hour after hour I ink tiny lines until the full length and breadth of the lineage courses through me.

As I pen each name, I imagine their lives: their weariness and tears, their confusion and doubt, their struggles and moments of despair, and their moments of clarity, serenity, freedom, and delight.

I recall the Buddha's words to his followers: "It is possible," he tells them. "If it were not possible, I would not ask you to do it." I imagine them, like me: brimming with tender, anticipatory faith; fallible, vulnerable, hopeful, unsure. With puffy knees, stiff fingers, and tired eyes, I am buoyed. It is possible to chart a path through pain and ignorance. It is possible to transform misery into gold. It is possible. Alchemy happens. But the process of transformation is not easy or effortless. It demands a whole-bodied, wholehearted engagement. No part left out.

When the lineage charts are completed, the heart of the ceremony begins.

In the dark of the night, we enter a womblike tent made of rich, ruby-colored velvet. Everything is red. The walls of the tent, the chair where I take my seat, the intensity of the moment.

I perch on an ornate throne, circled by three women in long black robes, none of whom stands over five foot two. They circumambulate me, creating a living web; chanting blessings, singing out their warmth and appreciation and thanks. Candles flicker, casting long shadows and golden light. We all glisten with sweat. Brooklyn is in the midst of a heat wave, and the AC at the Zen center has died. Outside, the traffic rumbles and the sky spreads wide. Inside we are transported into a timeless expanse of wilderness, far, far away.

The chanting stops and I rise. We stand facing each other in a circle. "For thousands of years our lineage has been a patriarchal one...." Yet we have always been here. Eternal and strong and true. We have always come together in this way, to sing and to celebrate, to reveal the power of our unshakable tenacity and joy. "For thousands of years women have also carried the dharma...." We have stood together as we stand together now, unapologetic and resolute, calling out into the crimson night.

Dharma transmission is a birthing. Within a circle of warm hands and warm hearts, fresh life is brought forth. The old is shed and something new emerges. Tonight, that something new is me. My solitary, fleshy body transformed. The tightly held drop of the person I have known melts and becomes an ocean. Wave upon wave of wonder wash through me.

Afterward I cannot stop grinning. A hollow ache I never knew I carried fills with quiet confidence. The deep torque inside me unwinds. My ribcage spreads and opens. I amble home through the streets of the city, lit and laughing.

Six weeks after the ceremony, Teah and I meet again. She carries an ease and fluidity that comes from being released of responsibility. "Done is what needed to be done," the Buddha declared after his awakening, calling out to the empty wind and sky. Her task, too, is finished. She has completed the ceremony, passed the baton, kept the flame of the lineage alive. She is breezy and lighter on her feet; her arms swing loose; her eyes are tender and bright.

We lower ourselves into the churning hot bubbles and exhale.

"We did it," she says, with a wide smile.

"Yes we did."

"It took five years," she tells me.

"Really? No!"

"Yep. I remember. It was five years ago that I mentioned transmission to you for the first time. I said it lightly, almost as a throwaway line."

Her words call up the memory: a blaze that landed in my chest and burned through me with wild, quiet yearning.

I shake my head in disbelief. "Five years," I say.

"I was just planting a seed," she explains. "I knew I needed to go slow so I wouldn't spook you. Every year or so, I'd mention it again; planting, planting along the way."

I let myself sink under the water and come up rubbing my eyes. "You saw something I couldn't see," I say, as much to myself as to her.

"Yep," she replies with a chuckle.

I feel cords of embarrassment and gratitude twine inside me. I am thankful for being seen but also chagrined at having my blindness exposed. I have always been intensely self-reliant, proud of my self-awareness, and reluctant to admit my dependence and needs. But here it all is in full bloom—the raw blossom of my vulnerability laid bare.

We shower and towel off, covering soft skin with clothes as we prepare to reenter the day. I reel in the understanding that there is no way to recover what has been revealed. And I am deeply grateful for it.

Nothing has changed. But everything is different. She extended a hand, and I took it. Our twined fingers became a bridge, and I agreed to cross it. I still don't know where it will lead, but I know I will continue walking.

I walk out of the gym with steadiness and contentment, a sureness in my gait; the courage to speak up when I might have stayed silent, and the poise to remain silent when there is no need to speak. I carry her seeing in my seeing. I carry her vision in my bones. I carry the simple truth of knowing: I do not walk alone.

My dharma transmission ceremony was the first of its kind. To date I am the only non-priest in the Suzuki Roshi lineage with authorization to offer the precepts in a *jukai* ceremony. I felt the weight of this role during the months leading up to the ceremony. Some days I awoke feeling eager about initiating something necessary and new. But many mornings I awoke anxious, heavy with dread. I felt pinched between bowing down and rising up; caught in the tangle of my respect for long-held traditions, the necessity to challenge them, and the risk of invoking ire from people I loved.

In Japanese, lay ordination is called *zuike tokudo*, "receiving the precepts and staying at home," while priest ordination is *shukke tokudo*, "receiving the precepts and leaving home." Soto Zen lay practitioners in Japan who complete *zuike tokudo* continue to live at home, fully engaged with family and work, while Soto Zen priests who complete *shukke tokudo* function as clergy. Japanese priests traditionally shave their heads, complete monastic training, tend the temple, and dedicate themselves to conducting rituals and ceremonies and to ministering to the local community.

With the unfolding of Zen practice in the West over the past four decades, many of these distinctions have blurred. Both lay practitioners and priests do monastic training, and priests and laypeople both teach classes and lead retreats. Most lay people do not conduct ceremonies such as births, deaths, marriages, or ordinations. But some do. And laypeople do not head temples or act as clergy, but many lay teachers lead sitting groups and minister to their communities.

In the epilogue of *Zen Mind Beginner's Mind,* Suzuki Roshi says, "American students are not priests and yet not completely laymen. I understand it this way: that you are not priests is an easy matter, but that you are not exactly laymen is more difficult. I think you are special people and want some special practice that is not exactly priest's practice and not exactly laymen's practice. You are on your way to discovering an appropriate way of life."

We are still finding our way into discovering what that means.

What does it take to chart a path straight through the messy, dynamic center of things? Is it possible to engage fully in the world with open hands and an open heart without being swallowed up by it? I didn't know the answer when I left the monastery, and I still don't know. But I knew then, as I know now: I want to find out.

One of my favorite images from Zen describes this birthing process as a simultaneous pecking in and pecking out. Picture an egg. Inside is a chick, gestating, waiting until it is mature enough to be released from its shell. Outside is a mother hen, listening, waiting until she is confident the chick is prepared to be free. When the baby chick is ready, it taps the shell from the inside. *Tap, tap.* When the mother hears the chick tapping, she taps in return. *Tap, tap.* Tapping in and tapping out. Hen and chick, teacher and student, parent and child, me and you, us and them. We listen and tap and wait, until, tap by tap, we crack our shells wide open.

This is how the journey unfolds. This is how the sky widens. We listen. We tap. We wait. And something new is born. We don't control what will happen. We don't get to say what or who will emerge. It is not our job to assess the outcome. It is our job to celebrate and appreciate.

Life itself tells the story. Our role is to wholeheartedly play our part.

BODHISATTVA VOWS
AND PRECEPTS

Bodhisattva Vows

Beings are numberless, I vow to free them.
Dharma gates are boundless, I vow to enter them.
Delusions are inexhaustible, I vow to cut through them.
Buddha's way is unsurpassable, I vow to become it.

Bodhisattva Precepts

I vow to refrain from doing harm.
I vow to do all that is good.
I vow to live for the benefit of all beings.

I vow not to kill, but to cherish all life.
I vow not to take what is not given, but to respect others' property.
I vow not to engage in improper sexuality, but to sustain love and care in my intimate relationships.
I vow not to lie, but to speak honestly and truthfully.
I vow not to intoxicate self or others, but to keep the mind clear.
I vow not to gossip, but to speak with sympathy and understanding.
I vow not to praise myself and condemn or blame others, but to be humble.

I vow not to covet, envy, or be jealous, but to give freely where needed.

I vow not to be angry, but to cultivate calm and peace.

I vow not to misuse the Triple Treasure—Buddha, Dharma and Sangha—but to cherish and uphold them.

NAMES OF FEMALE ANCESTORS CHANTED IN SOTO ZEN TEMPLES

Acharya Mahapajapati Acharya Mitta Acharya Yasodhara Acharya Tissa Acharya Sujata Acharya Sundari-nanda Acharya Vaddhesi Acharya Patachara Acharya Visakha Acharya Singalaka-mata Acharya Khema Acharya Uppalavanna Acharya Samavati Acharya Uttara Acharya Chanda Acharya Uttama Acharya Bhadda Kundalakesa Acharya Nanduttara Acharya Dantika Acharya Sakula Acharya Siha Acharya Dhammadinna Acharya Kisagotami Acharya Ubbiri Acharya Isidasi Acharya Bhadda Kapilani Acharya Mutta Acharya Sumana Acharya Dhamma Acharya Chitta Acharya Anopama Acharya Sukka Acharya Sama Acharya Utpalavarna Acharya Shrimala Devi Acharya Congchi Acharya Lingzhao Acharya Moshan Liaoran Acharya Liu Tiemo Acharya Miaoxin Acharya Daoshen Acharya Shiji Acharya Zhi'an Acharya Huiguang Acharya Kongshi Daoren Acharya Yu Daopo Acharya Huiwen Acharya Fadeng Acharya Wenzhao Acharya Miaodao Acharya Zhitong Acharya Zenshin Acharya Zenzo Acharya Ezen Acharya Ryonen Acharya Egi Acharya Shogaku Acharya Ekan Acharya Shōzen Acharya Mokufu Sonin Acharya Myosho Enkan Acharya Ekyu Acharya Eshun Acharya Soshin Acharya Soitsu Acharya Chiyono

RESOURCES ON
BUDDHIST WOMEN

I am grateful to the many people who have helped uncover the often over-looked or forgotten stories of Buddhist women, past and present. Here is a partial list of books presenting those stories.

Allione, Tsultrim. *Women of Wisdom.*

Batchelor, Martine. *Women on the Buddhist Path.*

Caplow, Frances, and Susan Moon. *Being Bodies: Women on the Paradox of Embodiment.*

———. *The Hidden Lamp: Stories from Twenty-Five Centuries of Awakened Women.*

Feldman, Christina. *Women Awake: Women Practicing Buddhism.*

Friedman, Lenore. *Meetings with Remarkable Women: Buddhist Teachers in America.*

Garling, Wendy. *Stars at Dawn: Forgotten Stories of Women in the Buddha's Life.*

Gross, Rita. *Buddhism after Patriarchy.*

Manuel, Zenju Earthlyn. *The Way of Tenderness: Awakening through Race, Sexuality and Gender.*

Murcott, Susan. *First Buddhist Women: Poems and Stories of Awakening.*

Palmo, Tenzin. *Buddhism through American Women's Eyes.*

Schireson, Grace. *Zen Women: Beyond Tea Ladies, Iron Maidens and Macho Masters.*

Starr, Mirabai. *Wild Mercy, Living the Fierce and Tender Wisdom of the Women Mystics.*

Thanissara. *Time to Stand Up.*

Thanissara and Kittisaro. *The Listening Heart.*

Tillsdale, Sallie. *Women of the Way: Discovering 2,500 Years of Buddhist Wisdom.*

Weingast, Matty, and Bhikkhuni Anandabodhi. *The First Free Women: Poems of the Early Buddhist Nuns.*

Willis, Jan. *Dharma Matters.*

———. *Dreaming Me: Black, Baptist and Buddhist—One Woman's Spiritual Journey.*

APPRECIATION AND
ACKNOWLEDGMENTS

Writing memoir is more than just reporting facts. It is crafting a slice of a story from a particular time, place, and perspective. There are many stories I could have told. The one told here—my journey in Soto Zen over three decades—is not the entirety of my spiritual path, but a tender, potent piece of it.

My spiritual journey has zigzagged through multiple traditions. After twelve years of intensive Zen practice, I sat many long retreats in the Insight (Vipassana) tradition, and I completed five years of teacher training through Spirit Rock Meditation Center, where I sit on the Teachers' Council, lead retreats, and co-lead the Community Dharma Leader program. My Insight training deepened and expanded my understanding, and it grounded my work of bringing mindfulness into organizations. My understanding was also influenced by years of Mahamudra practice and by twelve years as a student of the Diamond Approach, a brilliant psychospiritual teaching that helped me integrate and metabolize historical and emotional experience, introduced me to interactive inquiry, and illuminated the ongoing, ever-unfolding nature of awareness and awakening.

Each path offers unique gifts. Each has transformed my life. I am grateful for them all. With love and appreciation, I offer deep bows to the many wise and generous teachers who have supported me along the way: Yvonne Rand, Paul Haller, Tenshin Reb Anderson, Teah Strozer, Gil Fronsdal, Jack Kornfield, Sayadaw U Tejaniya, Venerable Analayo, Lama Palden, Sandra Maitri, and Hameed Ali.

Myriad hands and hearts helped nurture and birth this book. I am especially indebted to: Roger Housden, my first writing teacher; Leslie Keenan, writing coach extraordinaire; Stephany Evans, my fabulous agent; my dear dharma sister, Diana Winston, who introduced me to both Leslie and Stephany and who coined the term "ordinary bodhisattva"; my friend and writing buddy, Sebene Selassie, whose keen intellect and big heart kept me honest and inspired; my oldest friend and magnificent editor, Lisa Webster, who completely reshaped my shitty first draft and then polished all the sentences; to readers of the manuscript in its various iterations who shared their insights and input—Rachel Robasciotti, Allison Post, Greg Snyder, Laura O'Laughlin, Sandra Maitri, and Jeannine Jourdan (who suggested the addition of the appendixes at the end of the book); to Thanissara, Ayya Anandabodhi, and Ayya Santacitta for their priceless feedback on chapters 9 and 10; to Aya Cash and Josh Alexander, whose earnest encouragement kept me afloat while the manuscript was out to bid; and to the crew at North Atlantic Books—Shayna, Tim, Emily, Trisha, and Bevin—who believed in the book and shared their dedication and talent to turn it into something tactile and tangible.

To companions, colleagues, and inquiry partners whose love and care remind me of how paltry life would be without friendship and connection: Lara Heller, Maura Singer Williams, Lisa Webster, Diana Winston, Andrew Greenberg and Miriam Mousiaoff, Jeannine Jourdan, Julie Staples, Janice Jacobsen, Lauren Taylor, Erin Treat, and DaRa Williams.

To Todd Pierce and Cindy Elkins, whose vision and leadership lit the PEP torch; and to the PEP team—Ruben Rodriguez, Jennifer Nash, Anna Beusalink, Greg Gillis, Heather Neely, Robin Rorex, Robin Parker-Meredith, and Therese Tong—whose big hearts and hard work keep that torch burning.

To the indomitable Kimrenee Nash, Queen of Operations, whose dedication makes everything run smoothly behind the scenes.

To my courageous IDK and WE-R Circle sisters who have helped open, soften, and ripen me.

To my beloved Eugene, who has walked the path with me hand in hand all these years—I love you very much.

And to my little dog, Grover, who is always happy to see me, no matter what.

INDEX

Index

ABOUT THE AUTHOR

PAMELA WEISS is a Buddhist teacher authorized in two traditions—Zen and Theravada—and is the first and only layperson in the Suzuki Roshi Soto Zen lineage to receive full dharma transmission. After living as a monastic at Tassajara Zen monastery, she completed comprehensive training through Spirit Rock Meditation Center to become an Insight meditation teacher. She is a member of the Spirit Rock Teacher Council, a guiding teacher at San Francisco Insight, and a visiting teacher at the Brooklyn Zen Center. Weiss is also an executive coach, CEO, entrepreneur, and pioneer in bringing Buddhist principles and practices into the workplace. She lives in San Francisco with her husband and her little dog, Grover.

About North Atlantic Books

North Atlantic Books (NAB) is an independent, nonprofit publisher committed to a bold exploration of the relationships between mind, body, spirit, and nature. Founded in 1974, NAB aims to nurture a holistic view of the arts, sciences, humanities, and healing. To make a donation or to learn more about our books, authors, events, and newsletter, please visit www.northatlanticbooks.com.

North Atlantic Books is the publishing arm of the Society for the Study of Native Arts and Sciences, a 501(c)(3) nonprofit educational organization that promotes cross-cultural perspectives linking scientific, social, and artistic fields. To learn how you can support us, please visit our website.